ONE POT ITALIAN

MORE THAN 85
EASY, AUTHENTIC RECIPES

MASSIMO CAPRA

Photographs by Christopher Campbell

D1455799

A Sellers Publishing/Madison Press Book

Published by Sellers Publishing, Inc.

161 John Roberts Road, South Portland, Maine 04106
For ordering information:
(800) 625-3386 toll free
(207) 772-6814 fax

Visit our Web site: www.sellerspublishing.com
Email: rsp@rsvp.com

President and Publisher: Ronnie Sellers
Publishing Director: Robin Haywood
Senior Editor: Megan Hiller

ISBN 13: 978-1-4162-0763-4
Library of Congress Number: 2008909479

10 9 8 7 6 5 4 3 2 1

Produced by
Madison Press Books
1000 Yonge Street, Suite 200
Toronto, Ontario
M4W 2K2
madisonpressbooks.com

Printed in Singapore
by Imago Productions (F.E.) Ltd., Singapore

table of contents

acknowledgments

4

I must confess that when we decided to create this cookbook, I thought it could be done very easily. Wrong! Without the help of some very dedicated people, this would have been an impossible task. So, I want to thank the wonderful supporters who helped to make it all happen.

My deepest thanks go to:

My soulmate and wife, Rosa, for her encouragement and hard work troubleshooting, recreating and testing all of the recipes.

My sons, Andrew and Daniel, for eating everything I make with such gusto. Special thanks to Andrew for the wonderful photographs that appear throughout the book and on the cover.

My business partner, Paolo Paolini, for generously giving me the time to invest in this book and for wearing his heart on his sleeve.

The staff at Mistura and Sopra for looking after the restaurants (and me) so well. Special thanks to Peter Sananagan for running around gathering ingredients for the photography.

Marilyn Denis and the producers of "Cityline with Marilyn Denis" for inviting me to be on the show. My constant search for simple recipes to share with viewers resulted in this book.

The producers and crew of "Restaurant Makeover" for giving me fresh perspective and keeping me inspired with new ideas for my craft.

The freelance professionals and staff at Madison for guiding me to make the best book possible: Christopher Campbell and Dennis Wood for beautiful food photographs; Judy Phillips for smooth sentences; Kerry Plumley and Diana Sullada for tasteful art direction; Alison Maclean for clearing up my anxiety and keeping me on track; and special thanks to Al Cummings for believing in me and being there whenever I need him.

The patrons of my restaurants for understanding the beauty and simplicity of honest food, and for your constant support.

And my parents, who have my loving thanks and to whom I dedicate this book.

Un abbraccio a tuttti,

Massimo Capra
June 1, 2007

zuppe e minestre / soups

ribollita
tuscan cabbage soup

Ribollita is one of the most popular Tuscan soups. I turn to it whenever I'm in need of some soul food. This is a great soup to make ahead of time, as it can be frozen and reheated later without compromising the flavor.

Note: Soak the navy beans overnight in cold water. Rinse well under cold running water before using. Alternatively, do a quick soak by bringing the beans to a boil, turning off the heat, and letting stand for 1 hour.

Makes 8 servings

2 tbsp/30 mL extra-virgin olive oil	2 large tomatoes, chopped
4 cloves garlic, finely chopped	2 tsp/10 mL chopped fresh thyme or $\frac{1}{2}$ tsp/2 mL dried thyme
4 bay leaves	$\frac{1}{4}$ tsp/2 mL salt
1 large onion, finely chopped	$\frac{1}{2}$ tsp/1 mL freshly ground black pepper
2 large carrots, peeled and diced	
1 stalk celery, diced	$\frac{1}{2}$ loaf Italian bread, cut into $\frac{1}{2}$-inch (1 cm) slices (about 16 slices)
8 cups/2 L vegetable stock or water	
1 cup/250 mL dried navy beans, presoaked	$\frac{1}{2}$ cup/160 mL freshly grated Parmesan cheese
3 cups/750 mL shredded cabbage	

Heat the olive oil in a large saucepan over medium heat. Sauté the garlic and bay leaves for 3 minutes. Add the onion, carrot, and celery, and cook for 4 minutes, or until softened. Add the beans and the vegetable stock or water and bring to a boil. Reduce the heat and simmer for 40 minutes, or until the beans are tender. Stir in the cabbage, tomatoes, thyme, salt, and pepper. Simmer for 5 minutes, then remove the bay leaves.

In the meantime, preheat the oven to 350°F (180°C). Toast the bread slices for 15 minutes, or until lightly browned.

Pour a third of the bean mixture into a 13x9-inch (3 L) baking dish. Top with half of the bread slices. Repeat the layers, ending with the bean mixture and making sure all the bread is moistened. Sprinkle with Parmesan. Bake for 45 minutes, or until the top is bubbling and golden brown.

risi e bisi
rice and pea soup

This soup is a springtime favorite in Italy's Veneto region. Many people know this dish as a risotto, but it is really more of a thick soup. The tender, sweet peas are delicious to bite into, and the chicken broth offers an extra layer of flavor that will keep you coming back for more.

Makes 4 servings

2 tbsp/30 mL butter

2 tbsp/30 mL chopped onion

6 oz/170 g pancetta, chopped

12 oz/340 g shelled fresh green peas

8 cups/2 L chicken stock

$3\frac{1}{2}$ cups/875 mL vialone nano or other risotto rice

$\frac{1}{2}$ cup/125 mL chopped Italian parsley

salt and pepper

1 cup/250 mL grated grana padano cheese

Melt 1 tbsp/15 mL of the butter in a large skillet over medium heat. Add the onion and pancetta and sauté until soft. Stir in the peas and cook for about 1 minute, then add the chicken stock and bring to a boil.

Add the rice and parsley and simmer until the rice is cooked but still firm to the bite, about 14–17 minutes. The mixture should look dense, but with more liquid than a risotto. Season to taste with salt and pepper.

Remove from heat and gently stir in the remaining 1 tbsp/15 mL butter and the grana padano. Serve at once.

pappa al pomodoro
tuscan tomato soup

If you think that making soup is difficult, this recipe will change your mind. The key to this soup is the quality of the tomatoes. This recipe calls for canned tomatoes—buy the best quality possible. But use fresh, ripe red tomatoes when they're in season, or experiment by using yellow or orange tomatoes.

Makes 4–6 servings

4 tbsp/60 mL extra-virgin olive oil

1 large onion, finely chopped

4 cloves garlic, crushed

3 cups/750 mL canned plum (Roma) tomatoes, seeds removed

2 cups/500 mL vegetable stock

salt and pepper

2 cups/500 mL diced country-style white bread, preferably stale

1 bunch basil, chopped

grated Parmigiano-Reggiano or pecorino cheese, for garnish

extra-virgin olive oil, for garnish

Heat the olive oil in a stockpot over medium heat. Add the onion and garlic; sauté until the onion is translucent. Add the tomatoes and cook for 3–4 minutes to blend the flavors. Pour in the stock and simmer for 15 minutes.

Season to taste with salt and pepper. Stir in the bread and basil, and cook until the bread has a creamy consistency.

Serve with a generous sprinkle of grated Parmigiano-Reggiano or pecorino and a drizzle of extra-virgin olive oil.

Variation 1

Substitute 1 cup/250 mL of heavy cream for the bread, and blend the soup until smooth before adding the basil. This version is a favorite with kids.

Variation 2

For a clear, light tomato soup, use rice or pasta instead of bread.

Variation 3

For a great minestrone, just add chopped vegetables of your choice and simmer until they are cooked through.

zuppa di castagne
chestnut soup

This unusual but elegant soup is a good choice for a special dinner when you want to impress your guests, but it also makes a satisfyingly rib-sticking, eat-beside-the-fire kind of soup—terrific with garlic toast. Chestnuts are simple to roast, but if you prefer, buy vacuum-packed chestnuts that have already been roasted.

Note: To roast the chestnuts, soak them first in water for 2 hours. Score and roast in a 500°F (260°C) oven for 7–10 minutes. Once they are cool enough to touch, shell them—the shell and brown skin should come off easily.

Makes 4–6 servings

2 tbsp/30 mL extra-virgin olive oil	2 bay leaves
½ cup/125 mL diced pancetta	4 cups/1 L chicken stock
2 cloves garlic, crushed	extra-virgin olive oil and Parmigiano-Reggiano cheese, for garnish
1 cup/250 mL finely diced onion	
½ cup/125 mL finely diced celery	OR
½ cup/125 mL finely diced carrot	sour cream and chopped chives, for garnish
4 cups/1 L roasted chestnuts, skinned	

Heat the olive oil in a large stockpot over medium heat. Add the pancetta, garlic, onion, celery, and carrots, and sauté until the vegetables are translucent. Add 3 cups/750 mL of the roasted chestnuts along with the bay leaves and chicken stock, and simmer for 15 minutes.

Remove the soup from the heat, discard the bay leaves, and puree in a blender. Strain to refine the soup and remove any hard pieces of chestnut.

Return the strained soup to the heat, add the remaining 1 cup/250 mL of chestnuts, and simmer for another 5 minutes.

Serve with a sprinkle of extra-virgin olive oil and grated Parmigiano-Reggiano, or with a dollop of sour cream and chopped chives.

minestrone di massimo
massimo's fall harvest vegetable soup

Every cook has his or her own style of minestrone. Here's mine, with lots of soft, colorful, and sweet autumn vegetables. The only rule that applies to this soup is the way the vegetables are cut—it will influence the soup's look and the way it feels to the palate. Cut the vegetables quite small so that there is a variety in every spoonful. This recipe calls for six cloves of garlic, but feel free to add even more if you like.

Makes 6–8 servings

6 cloves garlic, crushed

4 tbsp/60 mL olive oil

1 cup/250 mL minced onion

1 cup/250 mL sliced celery hearts (tender innermost stalks)

1 cup/250 mL sliced carrot

1 cup/250 mL seeded and diced green and yellow zucchini

1 sprig fresh thyme

4 bay leaves

6 cups/1.5 L vegetable stock

salt and pepper

1 cup/250 mL red kidney beans, precooked or canned

1 cup/250 mL sliced leeks, including part of the green

1 cup/250 mL squash or pumpkin diced into ½-inch (1 cm) cubes

2 cups/500 mL shredded Savoy cabbage

½ cup/125 mL coarsely chopped Italian parsley

extra-virgin olive oil, for garnish

grated cheese of your choice, for garnish

In a stockpot over medium heat, sauté the garlic in the olive oil. Before the garlic browns, add the onion, celery, carrot, zucchini, thyme, bay leaves, and vegetable stock. Simmer for half an hour, or until the vegetables are soft. Season to taste with salt and pepper and add the kidney beans, leeks, squash or pumpkin, and cabbage. Simmer for 15 minutes.

To serve, top with the parsley, a drizzle of olive oil, and a handful of grated cheese of your choice.

minestra di riso e zucca
squash and rice soup

All summer I wait expectantly for the squash or pumpkin plants to bear their fruit. And is it ever worth the wait! I use squash in all sorts of dishes, from risotto to ravioli, from panna cotta to sautéed squash chips. And in soups, of course.

Makes 6–8 servings

1 tbsp/15 mL extra-virgin olive oil	2 bay leaves
1 tbsp/15 mL butter	2 lb/1 kg Hubbard or other dry squash, diced
1 cup/250 mL minced onion	
1 cup/250 mL minced carrot	8 cups/2 L light chicken stock
1 cup/250 mL minced celery	salt and pepper
1 cup/250 mL minced Swiss chard (silverbeet)	2 cups/500 mL vialone nano or other risotto rice
1 tsp/5 mL minced garlic	grated grana padano cheese, for garnish

Heat the olive oil and butter in a large stockpot over medium heat. Add the onion, carrot, celery, Swiss chard (silverbeet), garlic, and bay leaves, and sauté for about 1 minute. Stir in the squash and chicken stock. Simmer for 20 minutes.

Skim off the foam that forms on the top; season the soup to taste with salt and pepper. Add the rice and cook, stirring occasionally to prevent sticking, until tender but still firm, about 14–17 minutes.

Serve in bowls with a generous sprinkling of grated grana padano.

canederli alla trentina
tyrolean bread-dumpling soup

It would be wonderful if we could buy bread fresh every day, but that would probably mean too much left over. In many parts of Italy it is customary not to throw away leftover bread, but to grate it into homemade breadcrumbs, cook it in a custard as bread pudding, add it to soup as a thickening agent, or make it into dumplings, as in this recipe. Serve these dumplings in their cooking broth or with sage butter. Speck is a smoked boneless ham from south Tyrol.

Makes 4 servings

1 lb/500 g stale white bread	pinch of grated nutmeg
1 cup/250 mL milk	salt and pepper
1 tbsp/15 mL butter	5 cups/1.25 L chicken stock
4 oz/115 g speck, chopped	grated Parmigiano-Reggiano cheese, for garnish
3 cloves garlic, chopped	
1 cup/250 mL grated grana padano cheese	
2 eggs	**For sage butter:**
4 tbsp/60 mL chopped Italian parsley	12 whole sage leaves
1 tbsp/15 mL all-purpose (plain) flour	3 tbsp/45 mL butter

Chop the bread into small cubes and place in a medium bowl. Warm the milk and pour it over the bread. Let the bread steep in the milk for at least 2 hours.

Melt the butter in a skillet over medium heat. Add the speck and garlic; sauté gently until soft. Set aside to cool.

Add the grana padano and eggs to the bread mixture. Stir in the parsley, flour, and nutmeg, and season to taste with salt and pepper. Add the speck to the bread mixture and stir well; the mixture should be dough-like, soft and firm for easy handling, and sticky, not runny.

Bring the chicken stock to a gentle boil in a stockpot. In the meantime, dust your hands with flour to prevent sticking and roll the dough between your hands to form dumplings the size of golf balls. Drop the dumplings into the stock and simmer for 20 minutes, stirring occasionally to prevent sticking. Do not cook the dumplings at too rapid a boil or they will fall apart.

To prepare the sage butter, fry the sage leaves in the skillet with the butter until crisp. Add the dumplings, toss to coat, and serve at once with lots of grated Parmigiano-Reggiano.

zemino di ceci
genoa chickpea soup

When I was a boy in the 1960s, chickpeas seemed exotic to me; they are not used in traditional Italian recipes except perhaps as a snack. Sunday afternoons we spent at the cinema. Just before the movie began, an old man on a moped equipped with baskets front and rear would arrive in town to sell popcorn, lupini beans, and steaming hot cooked chickpeas, served salted in a paper cone. My treat was to buy a cola and a cone of chickpeas—nothing tasted as good to me in those days. Today I eat and cook with chickpeas quite often. This hearty soup is particularly nice in the autumn and winter.

Note: Soak the chickpeas overnight in a large bowl of cold water to soften, having first picked them over and discarded any stones or other particles. Rinse well under running water before using.

Makes 6–8 servings

3 cloves garlic, minced	2 cups/500 mL dried chickpeas, presoaked
1 cup/250 mL minced carrot	
1 cup/250 mL minced celery	8 cups/2 L chicken stock
1 cup/250 mL minced onion	salt and pepper
2 tbsp/30 mL extra-virgin olive oil	grated pecorino cheese, for garnish
2 bay leaves	garlic croutons, for garnish
2 cups/500 mL chopped Swiss chard (silverbeet)	

In a large pot, sauté the garlic, carrot, celery, and onion in the olive oil over medium heat until the vegetables are translucent. Add the bay leaves, Swiss chard (silverbeet), presoaked chickpeas, and stock. Simmer for 1½ hours. Season to taste with salt and pepper.

Serve in bowls with grated pecorino and garlic croutons sprinkled on top.

trippa con fagiolini dell'occhio
beef tripe soup with vegetables

Some people cringe at the thought of eating tripe, while others consider it a delicacy. In Cremona we eat this cold-weather dish mainly in osterie, tavern-like restaurants, as a small snack accompanied by a glass of good red wine. Once a year, at the beginning of autumn, it is a Cremona tradition to eat a bowl of tripe soup for good luck.

Note: Soak the black-eyed peas in cold water overnight. Rinse well under cold running water before using. Alternatively, do a quick soak by bringing the peas to a boil, turning off the heat, and letting stand for 1 hour.

Makes 4–6 servings

1 lb/500 g beef tripe	2 bay leaves
1 vanilla bean	2 tbsp/30 mL tomato paste
4 tbsp/60 mL white vinegar	2 cups/500 mL chopped tomatoes
5 cloves garlic, 4 left whole, 1 minced	6 cups/1.5 L chicken stock
pinch of salt	6 oz/170 g dried black-eyed peas, presoaked
3 tbsp/45 mL extra-virgin olive oil	
1 cup/250 mL minced onion	salt and pepper
1 cup/250 mL minced celery	½ cup/125 mL grated Parmigiano-Reggiano cheese
1 cup/250 mL minced carrot	

Wash the tripe thoroughly under cold running water. Cut into strips no longer than 2 inches (5 cm) and no wider than ½ inch (5 mm). Place the tripe in a pot of water with the vanilla bean, vinegar, 4 whole cloves of garlic, and pinch of salt; simmer for 15 minutes. Remove the tripe and set aside on a tray to cool.

Heat a stockpot over medium-high heat. Add the olive oil, minced garlic, onion, celery, carrot, and bay leaves; sauté for 5 minutes. Add the tripe and tomato paste and cook, stirring, for 1 minute. Stir in the tomatoes, chicken stock, and presoaked peas. Simmer until the tripe and the peas are tender, about 40 minutes. At this point the soup should be quite thick.

Season to taste with salt and pepper. Serve in individual bowls, with grated Parmigiano-Reggiano sprinkled on top, and accompanied by toasted garlic bread.

pasta e fagioli alla veneziana
bean and pasta soup venetian style

My father would eat romano beans only if they were shelled and skinned, which kept my mother busy for hours. You'll see that my father has greatly influenced this recipe—the beans don't need to be skinned. I recommend using fresh romano beans if they are available.

Makes 6–8 servings

2 tbsp/30 mL olive oil

2 tbsp/30 mL butter

2 cloves garlic, minced

2 cups/500 mL minced onion

1 cup/250 mL chopped pancetta

2 bay leaves

2 tbsp/30 mL tomato paste

8 cups/2 L light chicken stock, plus more as needed

2 lb/1 kg fresh romano beans (or 3 cups/750 mL drained canned romano beans)

salt and pepper

½ lb/250 g fresh fettuccine, cut into 2-inch (5 cm) pieces

extra-virgin olive oil, for garnish

grated grana padano cheese, for garnish

Heat the oil and butter in a cast-iron or other heavy-bottomed pot over medium heat. Add the garlic, onion, pancetta, and bay leaves, and sauté until the vegetables are soft and translucent. Stir in the tomato paste and cook a minute longer. Add the beans and stock, and simmer until the beans are cooked (about 20–30 minutes for fresh beans) or heated through (if using canned beans).

Scoop the beans out of the liquid and remove the bay leaves. Puree the beans in a food mill or food processor. Return the pureed beans to the stock and bring to a boil. The soup should be creamy but not too thick; add a bit of stock to thin it if necessary. Season to taste with salt and pepper.

Add the fettuccine and simmer, stirring frequently, until the pasta is cooked. Serve in bowls with a drizzle of olive oil and grated grana padano sprinkled on top.

insalate e uova / salads and eggs

"sfricasot" di mio papa
my father's scrambled eggs

My father loved preparing this dish, and it is one of the first dishes I learned to cook. It's simple to prepare—perfect after a long day at work or for a relaxed breakfast. These eggs are top of the line; they go well with smoked salmon, on toast with shaved truffle, or as a teaser with caviar, but also with a simple side salad.

Makes 4 servings

6 eggs	salt and pepper to taste
½ cup/125 mL grated Parmigiano-Reggiano cheese	1 tsp/5 mL olive oil
¼ cup/50 mL heavy cream	1 tsp/5 mL butter

Break the eggs into a bowl. Stir in the Parmigiano-Reggiano and cream. Season to taste with the salt and pepper.

Heat the olive oil and butter in a skillet (or use a nonstick skillet with no oil if you prefer) and pour in the egg mixture. With a heat-resistant spatula, scramble the eggs gently until cooked; they should be fluffy and light.

mortadella croccante all'occhio di bue
fried egg with crispy mortadella

If you like to play the "one-up" game with your food, try this instead of bacon and eggs. I don't need to tell you to buy the best Italian-style mortadella you can find, do I?

Makes 4 servings

1 tbsp/15 mL extra-virgin olive oil

1 large slice of mortadella,
½ inch (5 mm) thick

4 eggs

pepper

Heat the olive oil in a skillet over medium heat (or use a nonstick skillet with no oil if you prefer). Place the slice of mortadella in the pan and fry for about 1 minute, or until it starts to turn golden and crispy at the edges.

Flip the mortadella and immediately break the eggs on top of it. Season with pepper to taste and cover the pan with a lid, checking occasionally to make sure the mortadella isn't burning. Cook the eggs to your liking, and serve at once. ☞

frittata di mia mamma
my mother's frittata

If you go to Cremona, you may notice that the locals follow a routine: at about 11:00 AM they stop to have a snack and a glass of white wine or an aperitif. One of the many offerings at the bars is frittata. There is an art to frittata, and when it is made well, it can be difficult to stop at just one bite. Here is my mother's recipe.

Makes 8 servings

3 cups/750 mL spinach	1 cup/250 mL grated mild provolone cheese
3 cups/750 mL Swiss chard (silverbeet)	salt and pepper
2 green zucchini	2 tbsp/30 mL extra-virgin olive oil
12 eggs	2 tbsp/30 mL butter
1 cup/250 mL grated Parmigiano-Reggiano cheese	1 clove garlic, minced
	2 cups/500 mL julienned onion

Preheat oven to 350°F (180°C).

Wash the spinach and the Swiss chard (silverbeet) well, and boil or steam until tender. Squeeze out the excess water and chop coarsely. Cut the zucchini in half lengthwise and then into half-moons.

Break the eggs into a bowl and combine with the spinach, Swiss chard (silverbeet), Parmigiano-Reggiano, and provolone, mixing well to combine the eggs and loosen up the greens. Season to taste with salt and pepper.

Over medium heat, heat an oven-proof skillet; a 12-inch (30 cm) nonstick pan works best—you want the frittata to be at least 1½ inches (4 cm) thick. Add the olive oil and butter, zucchini, garlic, and onion, and sauté until the vegetables are soft and translucent. Add the egg mixture and stir well to incorporate it into the zucchini-onion mixture.

Place the pan in the oven and bake until the frittata is firm, about 10 minutes. The eggs are done when a toothpick inserted in the center of the frittata comes out dry.

Slide the frittata onto a plate, cut into wedges, and serve at once.

insalata di primavera
spring salad with asparagus, fiddleheads, and hazelnut vinaigrette

Springtime is the season for fiddleheads (fern shoots), ramp (wild garlic), asparagus, and peas. If you can't find fiddleheads, add some more asparagus, and cloves of garlic can be used instead of ramp.

Makes 4–6 servings

1 bunch white asparagus, tips only	1 cup/250 mL finely sliced shiitake mushrooms
1 bunch green asparagus, tips only	salt and pepper
1½ cups/375 mL fiddleheads, cleaned well	2 tbsp/30 mL sherry vinegar
1 cup/250 mL shelled fresh green peas	2 heads blond frisée (coral lettuce) or curly endive
1 bunch mini carrots, peeled	1 tbsp/15 mL hazelnut oil
1 tbsp/15 mL butter	2 tbsp/30 mL grapeseed oil
8 whole ramp, coarsely chopped	2 tbsp/30 mL toasted hazelnuts, for garnish

Steam or boil the asparagus tips, fiddleheads, green peas, and carrots.

Heat the butter in a skillet over medium heat. Add the ramp and mushrooms and sauté for 2 minutes. Season with salt and pepper, sprinkle with the sherry vinegar, and cook for 1 minute. Set aside.

Separate the lettuce leaves in a bowl. Add the steamed vegetables and the ramp-and-mushroom mixture. Whisk the hazelnut and grapeseed oils and season with salt and pepper. Dress the salad and arrange on individual plates. Top with cracked hazelnuts.

insalata di alberto
al's plaid salad

The idea of creating recipes to honor people, events, or places is not new. Although I can't remember exactly why, I know that this salad was created at Prego della Piazza for a play called *Forever Plaid* and named for Alberto, a very dear friend. The look and flavor combination of its ingredients is probably the reason why this salad always remained on the menu.

Makes 4–6 servings

1 cup/250 mL coarse sea salt	1 tbsp/15 mL red vine vinegar
1 white onion, skin left on	1 tbsp/15 mL vincotto vinegar
1 head radicchio	¼ cup/50 mL extra-virgin olive oil
2 bunches arugula (rocket)	salt and pepper
2 tomatoes	
1 cup/250 mL canned cannellini beans	

Preheat oven to 375°F (190°C).

Spread the sea salt over the bottom of an ovenproof dish, place the onion on top, and bake for 30–45 minutes.

Julienne the radicchio into ½-inch (5 mm) pieces and place in a serving bowl. Wash and dry the arugula (rocket) and add to the radicchio. Cut the tomatoes in half and remove the seeds, julienne into ½-inch (5 mm) pieces, and add to the bowl. Peel and julienne the baked onion and add to the bowl. Add the cannellini beans.

Whisk together the red wine vinegar, vincotto vinegar, olive oil, and salt and pepper. Dress the salad to taste, tossing well. ☺

insalata d'autunno
autumn salad with radicchio, red onion, and crispy shallots

Autumn is my favorite season in many ways. The scorching heat of summer is gone, the sun sets earlier, the fields yield the final harvest of the year, and the markets are filled with produce from local farms. This tasty salad calls for some of the best of the season's produce. It doesn't take a lot of time to prepare and it's sure to please. Sometimes I shave Parmigiano or asiago on top and have a bowl for lunch—it usually keeps me going until dinnertime.

Note: If you prefer, buy the shallots already fried; they're readily available in Asian markets and the Asian food section of supermarkets.

Makes 4–6 servings

For pickled red onion:

1 cup/250 mL water

1 cup/250 mL red wine vinegar

1/2 tsp/5 mL salt

1 tbsp/15 mL honey

2 medium red onions, julienned

For crispy shallots:

12 shallots, thinly sliced

4 tbsp/60 mL all-purpose (plain) flour

4 cups/1 L vegetable oil

pinch of salt

For salad:

1/2 head radicchio, julienned

1 Belgian endive, julienned

1/2 head escarole, julienned

1 medium blond frisée (coral lettuce), with bottom cut off to separate leaves

1 unpeeled green apple, julienned

1 cup/250 mL julienned carrots

2 plum (Roma) tomatoes, peeled, seeded, and julienned

2 tbsp/30 mL julienned pickled or raw red onion

4 tbsp/60 mL apple cider vinegar

4 tbsp/60 mL extra-virgin olive oil

salt and pepper

2 tbsp/30 mL toasted almonds

To prepare the pickled red onion, bring the water, red wine vinegar, salt, and honey to a boil in a small saucepan. Stir in the onion and bring back to a boil. Remove from the heat and let steep for 5 minutes. Strain and set aside, covered, until needed.

To prepare the crispy shallots, dredge the shallots in flour. Heat the vegetable oil to 285°F (140°C) and fry the shallots until crisp. Remove from the oil with a slotted spoon and drain on paper towels. Sprinkle with a pinch of salt.

To prepare the salad, toss together the radicchio, Belgian endive, escarole, blond frisée (coral lettuce), apple, carrot, tomato, and pickled or raw red onion in a bowl. Whisk together the apple cider vinegar, olive oil, salt, and pepper. Dress the salad to taste and toss well. Top with the crispy shallots and toasted almonds.

insalata d'estate
summer salad

Nothing beats a salad on a hot summer day—the ingredients are plentiful and at their prime, the combinations endless. I love to eat a big salad for dinner in the backyard with my feet up, watching the birds and waiting for the sunset. But, given the business I'm in, that's a rare occurrence, as summer is a busy season for the restaurant. Nevertheless, I still eat my summer salad.

Makes 4–6 servings

1 big handful French green beans (approximately 24)	1 cucumber, cut in half lengthwise, seeds removed
1 head Boston lettuce	4 tbsp/60 mL extra-virgin olive oil
1 head red leaf lettuce	1 tbsp/15 mL red wine vinegar
6 red radishes, thinly sliced	salt and pepper
4 green onions, chopped	1 avocado, peeled, pitted, and diced
2 medium carrots, finely julienned	2 tbsp/30 mL crumbled feta cheese (optional)
2 red tomatoes, cut in wedges	garlic croutons, for garnish

Boil the French beans in a pot of salted water to desired tenderness. In the meantime, toss together the Boston lettuce, red leaf lettuce, radishes, green onions, carrots, tomatoes, and cucumber in a large bowl. Add the cooked French beans.

Whisk together the olive oil, red wine vinegar, and salt and pepper to taste. Dress the salad, tossing lightly (spoons or clean hands, rather than tongs, work best), and divide onto individual plates. Top each with the avocado, crumbled feta, and hand-crumbled garlic croutons.

insalata belga e formaggio verde

belgian endive, roquefort, and pecan salad with pear vinaigrette

Makes 4 servings

For salad:

8 oz/225 g green beans

1 medium red onion

salt and pepper

extra-virgin olive oil, for seasoning

2 Belgian endives

1 bunch arugula (rocket)

2 Bosc pears, peeled, cored, and diced

8 oz/225 g crumbled Roquefort cheese

4 tbsp/60 mL toasted pecans or walnuts

For vinaigrette:

1 Bosc pear, peeled, cored, and diced

2 tbsp/30 mL rice vinegar

6 tbsp/90 mL light extra-virgin olive oil

salt and pepper

Preheat oven to 400°F (200°C).

Bring a pot of water to a boil. Add the green beans and cook until crisp-tender. Remove the beans and plunge into cold water to retain their color. Set aside.

Cut the onion in half crosswise and season with salt, pepper, and olive oil. Bake until tender, about 20 minutes. Set aside to cool, then cut into wedges.

Separate the endive leaves and mix with the arugula (rocket). Add the cooked green beans, onion wedges, pear, Roquefort, and pecans or walnuts.

For the vinaigrette, blend the pear, rice vinegar, olive oil, and salt and pepper to taste in a blender at high speed. Pour over the salad, toss well, and serve. ☗

insalata d'invèrno
winter salad with potatoes and apples

One day, many years ago, I got tired of making "spring mix" salad in winter, so I yanked the Caesar and mesclun salads from the menu and started making salads by the season. Doing so gave the kitchen a boost of creativity. This is one of the many combinations we created.

Note: Soak the radicchio in cold water overnight to remove bitterness.

Makes 4–6 servings

2 large potatoes	2 heads radicchio, washed and cut into small pieces
salt and pepper	
4 tbsp/60 mL cider vinegar	2 tbsp/30 mL chopped Italian parsley
2 crisp green apples	$\frac{1}{2}$ cup/125 mL shaved asiago cheese, for garnish
juice of 1 lemon	
4 tbsp/60 mL extra-virgin olive oil	2 tbsp/30 mL crispy bacon bits, for garnish
1 small sweet onion, julienned	

Cook the potatoes, skin on, in salted boiling water under fork-tender. Once they are cool enough to handle, remove the skins and dice the potatoes into 1-inch (2.5 cm) cubes. Dress immediately with salt, pepper, and 2 tbsp/30 mL cider vinegar. Dressing the potatoes while they are warm will make them very flavorful (this process can be done the day before if you wish).

Cut the apples into wide juliennes and sprinkle with lemon juice to prevent discoloring.

Heat 1 tbsp/15 mL olive oil in a skillet over high heat. Add the onion and toss rapidly to prevent scorching. Sprinkle with the remaining 2 tbsp/30 mL cider vinegar, cook for 2 minutes, and remove from heat.

In a medium bowl combine the potatoes, apples, radicchio, and parsley. Pour the onion-and-vinegar mixture on top and dress with salt, pepper, and the remaining 3 tbsp/45 mL olive oil, tossing gently to blend the flavors. To finish, divide the salad into individual bowls and sprinkle with shaved asiago and bacon bits.

panzanella toscana
tuscan bread salad

I spent five summers by the Tuscan seaside working in a small hotel. There I developed a friendship with the baker who supplied bread to the hotel. This very generous man frequently invited me to his house for a grigliata al fresco, or outdoor grill, where the wine flowed and the food was plentiful. It was here that I first tasted panzanella. Made with stale bread, this salad can be prepared ahead of time—great for picnics and summer buffets in the garden.

Makes 4–6 servings

1 lb/500 g chopped ripe tomatoes	4 tbsp/60 mL extra-virgin olive oil
1 cucumber, peeled, seeded, and chopped	2 tbsp/30 mL red wine vinegar
	salt and pepper
1 medium red onion, julienned	1 loaf crusty Italian bread, preferably stale
1 large bunch basil	
1 bunch mint	

Combine the tomatoes and cucumber in a bowl. Add the onion and the basil and mint leaves. Dress the tomato mixture with the olive oil, red wine vinegar, and salt and pepper to taste. Break the bread into small pieces by hand and add to the salad. Toss well and serve. ☞

insalata rossa
red salad

When I worked at Prego della Piazza, I was inspired by famed restaurateur Michael Carlevale. His passion for his craft was the drive behind every aspect of his life. "My customers," he explained to me, "are my guests, and this restaurant is my living room." Those were very good—but long—days. The restaurant opened at 11:30 AM and closed when the last guests had left, sometimes in the wee hours of the morning. On the menu were many salads, and this is one of the most popular. If radicchio di Treviso is unavailable, substitute red radicchio.

Makes 4 servings

2 medium beetroots	1 head radicchio di Treviso, chopped
2 red onions	8 soft oil-packed sun-dried tomatoes
salt	4 slices red tomato
extra-virgin olive oil, for seasoning	4 tbsp/60 mL extra-virgin olive oil
1 tsp/5 mL red vine vinegar	4 tsp/20 mL good balsamic vinegar
2 red peppers (capsicums), quartered	flaked sea salt and freshly ground black pepper

Preheat oven to 450°F (230°C).

Boil the beetroots in a pot of salted water until they are soft, about 30 minutes. Cool and peel. Slice crosswise into ½-inch (5 mm) slices and set aside.

Cut the onions in half crosswise and season with salt and a light sprinkling of olive oil—just enough to give the onions a shine. Place the onions on a small baking sheet and bake until soft, about 20 minutes. Remove from the oven and sprinkle with the red wine vinegar. Set aside to cool.

Turn the oven up to 500°F (260°C). Give the peppers (capsicums) a light sprinkling of olive oil and place them on the baking sheet; bake for about 15 minutes. Remove the peppers (capsicums) and put them in a plastic bag to steam; this will make removing the skins easy once they are cold.

To prepare the salad, arrange the radicchio on individual serving plates. Add, from right to left, the tomato slices, roasted peppers (capsicums), sun-dried tomatoes, beetroots, and roasted onions. To dress, sprinkle each salad with 1 tbsp/15 mL olive oil and 1 tsp/5 mL balsamic vinegar, sea salt, and freshly ground black pepper to taste.

risotto e polenta /
risotto and polenta

risotto ubriaco
drunken risotto

If you have heard of champagne risotto, then you will understand this recipe. I first encountered it in a restaurant in Venice, where it was made with Amarone. At first I thought it a waste of good wine, until I learned that using only the best-quality ingredients when preparing a recipe is as important as having the right drinking wine to accompany the dish.

Makes 4–6 servings

1 onion, finely chopped	2 cups/500 mL full-bodied red wine
4 cloves garlic, thinly sliced	6 cups/1.5 L light chicken stock
2 tbsp/30 mL vegetable oil	2 tbsp/30 mL butter
1 cup/250 mL smoked pork belly, diced into $\frac{1}{2}$-inch (5 mm) pieces	4 tbsp/60 mL grated Parmigiano-Reggiano cheese
$3\frac{1}{2}$ cups/875 mL carnaroli rice, unwashed	

Sweat the onion and garlic in the vegetable oil. Add the diced pork belly and stir to mix well.

Add the rice and toast it, stirring constantly to prevent sticking, for 2–3 minutes, until it is very hot but not browned. Pour in the wine and simmer until the liquid is absorbed or evaporated. Add enough chicken stock to cover the rice; simmer until the rice has absorbed most of the liquid, stirring frequently to prevent sticking. Continue to add the stock, a ladleful at a time, letting the rice absorb most of the liquid before adding more, until the rice is tender but firm. Be careful toward the end not to add too much stock—the risotto should be creamy, not soupy. This process should take 16–18 minutes in total.

When the rice is cooked, remove from the heat. Add the butter and Parmigiano-Reggiano; stir vigorously to fluff. Serve at once in bowls. ☺

risotto con asparagi bianchi, pepe nero e fragole
risotto with white asparagus, black pepper, and wild strawberries

The most important thing to remember when making risotto is to introduce a flavor that complements the rice—in this case, asparagus and strawberries. Don't worry about the asparagus not being crunchy; the more you cook it, the tastier it will be. Choose soft, fragrant strawberries. Feel free to use white or wild asparagus when in season.

Makes 4–6 servings

1 medium onion, finely chopped

2 tbsp/30 mL extra-virgin olive oil

1 bunch asparagus, cleaned, blanched, and diced

3½ cups/875 mL carnaroli rice, unwashed

½ cup/125 mL white wine

6 cups/1.5 L chicken or vegetable stock, preferably with an asparagus flavor

2 cups/500 mL ripe strawberries, diced

2 tbsp/30 mL butter

grated Parmesan cheese

grated zest of 1 lemon

aged balsamic vinegar, for garnish

In a heavy-bottomed pot over medium heat, sauté the onion in the olive oil. Add the asparagus and sauté for 2–3 minutes. Add the rice and toast it, stirring constantly to prevent sticking, for 2–3 minutes, until it is very hot but not browned.

Pour in the wine and simmer until it is absorbed or evaporated. Add two ladlefuls of stock and simmer gently, stirring frequently to prevent sticking, until the rice has absorbed most of the liquid. Continue adding the stock, a ladleful at a time, letting the rice absorb most of the liquid before adding more, until the rice is tender but firm. Be careful toward the end not to add too much stock—the risotto should be creamy, not soupy. This process should take 16–18 minutes in total.

When the rice is cooked, remove from the heat. Add the strawberries, butter, Parmesan, and lemon zest. Stir well and serve with aged balsamic vinegar drizzled around the edges.

risotto e polenta   risotto and polenta

risotto alle erbette e pecorino
herbed risotto with pecorino

For this risotto, the amount of greens you use will greatly affect the taste. For me, the more the better. The pecorino pepato (sheep's milk cheese with whole peppercorns) will also influence the taste, so use restraint when adding it.

Makes 4–6 servings

6 cups/1.5 L vegetable stock	$3\frac{1}{2}$ cups/875 mL vialone nano or other risotto rice, unwashed
1 onion, finely chopped	$\frac{1}{2}$ cup/125 mL white wine
4 cloves garlic, crushed	
2 tbsp/30 mL extra-virgin olive oil	2 tbsp/30 mL butter
2 bunches baby spinach, chopped	$\frac{1}{2}$ cup/125 mL grated pecorino pepato cheese
2 bunches Swiss chard (silverbeet), greens only, chopped	

Bring the stock to a boil, turn down the heat, and keep it at a simmer.

In a large sauté pan over medium heat, sweat the onion and garlic with the olive oil. Add the spinach and Swiss chard (silverbeet) and sauté until all the liquid has evaporated.

Add the rice, stir to coat, and let it toast for 2–3 minutes, stirring constantly. Pour in the wine and stir until it is absorbed or evaporated.

Add a ladleful of vegetable stock and stir frequently until the rice has absorbed most of the liquid. Continue adding the stock a ladleful at a time, letting the rice absorb most of the liquid before adding more, until the rice is tender but firm. Be careful not to let the rice dry out too much, but also be careful toward the end not to add too much stock—the risotto should be creamy, not soupy. This process should take 16–18 minutes in total.

When the rice is cooked, remove it from the heat. Add the butter and pecorino; stir vigorously to fluff. Serve immediately in bowls.

risotto alle rape rosse
red beet risotto

I began developing this recipe back in the 1980s at Prego della Piazza. My partner, Michael Carlevale, and I were experimenting with colored foods—red, green, yellow, orange. Making risotto has always been one of my strong suits, so the dish was a natural candidate for such experiments. Beetroots are one of my favourite vegetables, and so the recipe was born.

Makes 4–6 servings

2 cups/500 mL beetroot juice	3½ cups/875 mL carnaroli rice
1 onion, finely chopped	½ cup/125 mL white wine
4 cloves garlic, thinly sliced	4 cups/1 L vegetable stock
2 tbsp/30 mL vegetable oil	2 tbsp/30 mL butter
1 bunch beetroot greens, finely chopped	4 tbsp/60 mL grated Parmigiano-Reggiano cheese

Bring the beetroot juice to a boil and skim off the foam. Set aside to cool.

In a medium saucepan over medium heat, sauté the onion and garlic in the vegetable oil. Add the beetroot greens and stir well. Add the rice and stir to coat with the onion mixture.

Pour in the wine and stir until most of the liquid is absorbed or evaporated. Add about half the stock, a ladleful at a time, and simmer until the rice has absorbed most of it, stirring frequently to prevent sticking. Add the beetroot juice, 1 cup/250 mL at a time, and simmer until the rice has absorbed most of it. Continue adding stock one ladleful at a time. Be careful not to add too much stock; the risotto should be creamy, not soupy, and the rice should be tender but firm. This process should take 16–18 minutes in total.

When the rice is cooked, remove it from the heat and add the butter and Parmigiano-Reggiano. Serve at once in bowls. 🍲

polenta taragna
buckwheat and cheese polenta

North of Cremona lies the town of Bergamo. Bergamo's historic center is divided in two—the very old high city and the more modern lower city. You'll find top-notch restaurants and trattorie with wonderful local foods; my wife and I had this polenta dish in one of them and we absolutely loved it. Serve it with steamed vegetables or sautéed porcini mushrooms, or as a side dish with a pot roast or stew.

Makes 6–8 servings

4 cups/1 L water

salt

2 tbsp/30 mL extra-virgin olive oil

2 cups/500 mL coarse buckwheat flour

1 cup/250 mL yellow cornmeal polenta flour (preferably bergamasca)

2 cups/500 mL Bitto or casera cheese

2 tbsp/30 mL grated Parmigiano-Reggiano cheese

2 tbsp/30 mL stracchino cheese

Combine the buckwheat and polenta flours. In a medium pot, bring the water to a boil, salt to taste, and add the oil. Reduce the heat to low and gently whisk in the flours, adding as much as needed to make a paste-like consistency.

Simmer gently, stirring occasionally, for about 45 minutes. Remove from the heat and add the cheeses, stirring vigorously until the cheese becomes stringy. Serve at once. ☺

risotto con zucchine e scampi
scampi and zucchini risotto

Even though this is a seafood risotto, I like to use a light chicken stock. It makes the rice creamy and accentuates the flavors of the other ingredients, rather than masking them. I have tried using fish stock, but find the taste too strong.

Note: Zucchini can be pulpy, so I recommend slicing them in half lengthwise and scooping out the seeds before slicing them into half-moons.

Makes 4–6 servings

6 cups/1.5 L light chicken stock	3½ cups/875 mL carnaroli rice, unwashed
12 oz/340 g scampi	1 cup/250 mL white wine
1 cup/250 mL chopped onion	2 tbsp/30 mL butter
1 clove garlic, chopped	1 bunch Italian parsley, chopped
2 cups/500 mL zucchini, sliced into ½-inch (5 mm) half-moons	¼ cup/50 mL asiago cheese
2 tbsp/30 mL extra-virgin olive oil	

Bring the chicken stock to a boil. Meanwhile, shell and devein the scampi, reserving the shells. Once the stock has reached a boil, add the scampi shells and simmer.

In a heavy-bottomed pot over medium heat, sauté the onion, garlic, and zucchini in the olive oil until the vegetables are soft. Add the scampi and sauté lightly. Add the rice and let it toast for 2–3 minutes, stirring constantly to prevent sticking, until very hot but not browned.

Pour in the white wine and simmer until the liquid is absorbed or evaporated. Add two ladlefuls of chicken stock (without the scampi shells) and simmer gently, stirring occasionally to prevent sticking, until the rice has absorbed most of the liquid. Continue adding the stock, a ladleful at a time, letting the rice absorb most of the liquid before adding more, until the rice is tender but firm. Be careful toward the end not to add too much stock—the risotto should be creamy and dense, not soupy. This process should take 16–18 minutes in total.

When the rice is cooked, remove it from the heat and add the butter, parsley, and asiago. Stir well and serve.

risotto e polenta   risotto and polenta

polenta di castagne
chestnut polenta

October in Italy brings many festivals, most of them related to the autumn harvest of mushrooms, truffles, pumpkins, grapes, and, of course, chestnuts. I like to boil chestnuts and simply peel and eat them. Others in my family like them roasted.

This polenta is made with chestnut flour. Your local Italian food shop should carry it; if it doesn't, ask to have it brought in. This polenta has a sweet flavor and there are many ways to serve it. Try it with sautéed mushrooms or crispy bacon and fresh goat cheese or sautéed Brussels sprouts, cabbage, and pork or wild game stew.

Makes 4 servings

4 cups/1 L water

½ tsp/2 mL salt

1 tbsp/15 mL extra-virgin olive oil

1½ cups/425 mL chestnut flour, sifted

Bring the water, salt, and olive oil to a boil. Remove from heat and gently add the sifted flour, whisking constantly to prevent lumps. Once all the flour is incorporated, return the pot to the heat and simmer over low heat, stirring occasionally, for 10–15 minutes.

polenta di ceci "panella"
fried chickpea polenta

Panella is a Sicilian snack food that can be found in just about any friggitoria, or shop that specializes in fried foods. I first encountered it in my army days, when my Sicilian friends made it. Eat it between sliced bread with a sprinkling of salt or dressed with tomatoes and olive spread. Once fried, it can be used as a side dish with lamb or fish, or make it into croutons for salads instead of using bread.

Makes 26 panelle

3 cups/750 mL water	2 tbsp/30 mL minced Italian parsley
2½ cups/625 mL chickpea flour	2 tbsp/30 mL dried oregano
salt and pepper	6 cups/1.5 L vegetable oil

Pour the water into a medium saucepan and stir in the chickpea flour, whisking to break up any lumps. Season to taste with salt and pepper and cook over medium heat, stirring constantly, for about 15 minutes, until the mixture begins to pull away from the sides of the pan. Add the parsley and oregano and pour the mixture onto an oiled cookie sheet, spreading it out with a spatula to ½ inch (5 mm) thick. Set aside to cool completely, then cut into 2x3-inch (5x8 cm) rectangles.

In a frying pan, heat the vegetable oil to 375°F (190°C) and fry the polenta in batches; don't put too many in at one time, as that will lower the temperature of the oil. Fry until the panelle are golden brown, turning as necessary. Remove from the oil with a slotted spoon and drain on paper towels. Serve at once.

purè di fave e cicoria
fava bean polenta with chicory

Many years ago I visited the region of Puglia, on the heel of Italy. It was my first time there, and it was a great eating experience. Puglia is known for fruits and vegetables of all sorts, especially its olives. The region is surrounded by the sea and has terrific restaurants. One, in the town of Alberobello, served this dish accompanied by grilled country-style crusty bread, olive oil, and black olives. It was delicious in its simplicity.

Makes 4–6 servings

12 oz/340 g dried fava (broad) beans, soaked overnight

8 oz/225 g potatoes, peeled and diced

salt

1 lb/500 g fresh chicory or dandelion greens, chopped

1 cup/250 mL extra-virgin olive oil

¼ cup/175 mL infornate (baked) black olives, pitted

extra-virgin olive oil, for garnish

freshly ground black pepper

Place the soaked beans and potatoes in a saucepan. Add enough water to just cover the vegetables, season with ¼ tsp/2 mL salt, and bring to a boil. Lower the heat and simmer gently for about 15 minutes, checking occasionally and adding more water if the pan becomes too dry. The potatoes are cooked when soft, and the beans when they are falling apart.

Mash the bean-and-potato mixture with a wooden spoon or potato masher. Season to taste with salt.

Bring the chicory to a boil in salted water and cook for about 1 minute. Drain and add it to the mashed beans and potato.

Place one spoonful of the bean mixture on a plate and spread it out to cover the surface. Garnish with the olives and a generous pour of olive oil. Top with freshly ground black pepper and serve warm.

risotto con radicchio, pancetta e vincotto
risotto with radicchio, bacon, and vincotto

Why use radicchio only in salads? If you are concerned it will be too bitter, soak cleaned, cut radicchio overnight in cold water to remove the bitterness. There are several varieties of radicchio; the radicchio di Treviso called for in this recipe looks like red Belgian endive. You may substitute red radicchio if radicchio di Treviso is unavailable.

Pancetta is the Italian name for salt-cured bacon; it comes rolled or flat, roasted or smoked, double-smoked, or in many other forms. For this recipe, choose pancetta affumicata, or roasted bacon, which can be found in the deli section of most supermarkets. It is similar to regular bacon but contains less water.

Makes 4–6 servings

1 medium onion, finely chopped	3$\frac{1}{2}$ cups/875 mL vialone nano or other risotto rice, unwashed
8 oz/225 g pancetta affumicata (roasted bacon), cut into $\frac{1}{2}$-inch (1 cm) pieces	$\frac{1}{2}$ cup/125 mL white wine
3 cups/750 mL diced radicchio di Treviso	6 cups/1.5 L chicken stock
2 tbsp/30 mL vegetable oil	2 tbsp/30 mL butter
	2 oz/50 g asiago cheese, grated
	4 tbsp/60mL vincotto vinegar

In a heavy-bottomed pot over medium heat, sauté the onion, pancetta, and radicchio in the vegetable oil until soft.

Add the rice and toast it, stirring constantly to prevent sticking, for 2–3 minutes, until very hot but not browned. Pour in the wine and simmer until the liquid is absorbed or evaporated. Add two ladlefuls of chicken stock and simmer gently, stirring frequently to prevent sticking. Continue adding the stock, a ladleful at a time, letting the rice absorb most of the liquid before adding more, until the rice is tender but firm. Be careful toward the end not to add too much stock—the risotto should be creamy, not soupy. This process should take 16–18 minutes in total.

When the rice is cooked, remove it from the heat and add the butter and asiago. Spoon into bowls, drizzle 1 tbsp/15 mL of vincotto over each, and serve at once.

risotto del contadino
farmer's risotto

Try this recipe and you will learn my idea of comfort food. Risotto is not only tasty, it sticks to your ribs. This recipe in particular is very popular in my house. Don't add too much sausage—the idea is to eat a tasty risotto with a bit of meat in it, not sausage with rice on the side.

Makes 4–6 servings

6 cups/1.5 L chicken stock

1 small onion, finely chopped

2 tbsp/30 mL extra-virgin olive oil

7 oz/200 g sweet Italian sausage, skinned and crumbled

3$\frac{1}{2}$ cups/875 mL vialone nano or other risotto rice, unwashed

$\frac{1}{2}$ cup/125 mL white wine

$\frac{1}{3}$ cup/75 mL tomatoes, skinned, seeded, and diced into $\frac{1}{4}$-inch (5 mm) pieces

2 tbsp/30 mL butter

1 bunch Italian parsley, coarsely chopped

$\frac{1}{2}$ cup/125 mL grated grana padano cheese

Bring the chicken stock to a boil, then reduce heat to simmer.

In a large sauté pan over medium heat, sauté the onion in the olive oil. Add the sausage meat and rice and toast the rice for 2–3 minutes, stirring constantly to prevent sticking, until it is very hot but not browned. Pour in the white wine and simmer, stirring constantly, until the liquid is absorbed or evaporated.

As you continue to stir, add the chicken stock a ladleful at a time, each time letting the rice absorb most of the liquid before adding more. After about 10 minutes, add the tomatoes. Continue adding the stock a ladleful at a time, letting the rice absorb most of the liquid before adding more, until the rice is tender but firm. This process should take 16–18 minutes in total.

When the rice is cooked, remove it from the heat and add the butter, parsley, and grana padano. Stir vigorously, using a whipping motion, to fluff the risotto. Serve at once in bowls. 🍲

risotto e polenta   risotto and polenta

bottoni di pagliaccio
grilled polenta "clown's buttons" and sausage

You will have a hard time finding anyone in Cremona who doesn't eat salami. There's a type for every need, and the open-air market is overflowing with stands selling it. This recipe is made with thick Italian sausage and is a favorite in my house, not only because of the taste but also because of its whimsical name—clown's buttons—which is unique to Cremona. We often eat the polenta and sausage by itself as a snack, but it also makes a nice light meal if served with a salad.

Makes 4 servings

2 large Italian sausages	2 scallions, chopped
2 tbsp/30 mL extra-virgin olive oil, plus extra for dressing	1 lb/500 g cooked polenta
6 tbsp/90 mL red vine vinegar, plus extra for dressing	1 head escarole
	salt and pepper

Cut the sausages into coins and sauté in a skillet with 2 tbsp/30 mL of the olive oil until crisp on both sides. Pour in the red wine vinegar and cook until it evaporates. Sprinkle on the scallions and toss briefly to wilt them slightly.

Cut the polenta into disks. Grill or sauté in a pan until crisp on both sides.

Arrange the polenta and sausage coins in rings on a plate, leaving room in the center for the salad. Cut the escarole into bite-sized pieces and season to taste with salt, pepper, olive oil, and vinegar. Place in the center of the plate. ☞

risotto all'aragosta
lobster risotto

This risotto is a favorite at Mistura. Of all the ways we have created risotto with lobster, this is definitely my favorite.

Makes 4–6 servings

2 lobsters, weighing 1½ lb/0.5 kg each, or 12 oz/375 g canned or frozen lobster, with juices

8 cups/2 L light chicken stock

2 tbsp/30 mL extra-virgin olive oil

½ cup/125 mL chopped onion

6 fresh plum (Roma) tomatoes, peeled, seeded, and chopped, or 2 cups/500 mL canned tomatoes, chopped and drained

3½ cups/875 mL carnaroli rice, unwashed

½ cup/125 mL white wine

1 bunch basil, chopped

2 tbsp/30 mL butter

If using live lobsters, cook them in boiling salted water for 8 minutes; cool in ice water. Remove the meat and scrape the tomalley (liver) out of the body cavity; reserve the tomalley in a bowl. Cut the meat into ½-inch (1 cm) cubes and set aside.

Meanwhile, bring the chicken stock to a boil and reduce heat to a gentle simmer.

Heat the olive oil in a heavy-bottomed pot over medium heat. Sauté the onion. Add the tomalley and tomatoes; cook for 3–4 minutes. Add the rice and toast it, stirring constantly to prevent sticking, for 2–3 minutes, until it is very hot but not browned.

Pour in the white wine and simmer until the liquid is absorbed or evaporated. Add two ladlefuls of stock and simmer gently, stirring frequently, until the rice has absorbed most of the liquid. Continue adding the stock, a ladleful at a time, keeping the rice wet but letting most of the liquid absorb before adding more, until the rice is tender but firm. Be careful toward the end not to add too much stock—the risotto should be creamy, not soupy. This process should take 16–18 minutes in total.

When the rice is almost cooked, stir in the lobster meat (with juices, if using canned or frozen, for extra flavor to replace the tomalley) and basil. Remove from the heat, stir in the butter, and serve at once in bowls.

risotto e polenta   risotto and polenta

pasta / pasta

bigoli in salsa
spaghetti with anchovies

Bigoli are very thick noodles produced with machines called bigolaro or torchio. Bigoli are know in Italy under many names: in Tuscany they are called pici, farther south spaghettoni or strozzapreti. The sauce originated in Venice and the surrounding region, where it is customary to eat bigoli in salsa on Christmas Eve.

Makes 4–6 servings

1 lb/500 g bigoli or thick spaghetti	2 tbsp/30 mL tomato paste
2 tbsp/30 mL extra-virgin olive oil	2 cups/500 mL chopped, seeded tomatoes
1 medium onion, finely chopped	
2 cloves garlic, finely chopped	½ cup/125 mL water
8 oil-packed anchovies, chopped	½ tsp/5 mL chilli paste
	salt and pepper

Cook the pasta al dente in a big pot of boiling salted water.

In the meantime, heat the oil in a saucepan over medium heat. Sauté the onion for 1 minute. Add the garlic and chopped anchovies, and cook until the vegetables are translucent; the anchovies should break up during this process. Add the tomato paste and cook for 2–3 minutes. Add the tomatoes, water, chilli paste, and salt and pepper to taste, and simmer for about 15 minutes, stirring occasionally.

Drain the cooked pasta and toss with the tomato sauce. Serve at once.

spaghettini ai frutti di mare
spaghettini with seafood

This recipe is a crowd-pleaser. Make sure not to overcook the spaghettini, and let the seafood speak for itself—there's no need for heavy tomato or cream sauces.

Makes 4 servings

8 oz/225 g squid, cleaned (ask your fishmonger to clean it)	¼ cup/50 mL white wine (optional)
1 lb/500 g fresh clams	8 oz/225 g small shrimp, peeled and deveined
1 lb/500 g spaghettini	1 cup/250 mL diced tomatoes
3 tbsp/45 mL extra-virgin olive oil	1 tsp/5 mL dried oregano
1 clove garlic, sliced	salt and pepper
1 onion, finely chopped	4 tbsp/60 mL chopped Italian parsley

Rinse the squid and clams under cold running water to wash off any grit. Slice the squid into very thin rings, about ½ inch (5 mm) thick. Set both aside.

Boil the spaghettini al dente in a big pot of boiling salted water.

In the meantime, heat a skillet over medium heat. Add the oil, garlic, and onion; sauté until the vegetables are soft and translucent. Add the clams and wine, if using, and sauté until the clams have opened, about 3–4 minutes. Discard any clams that do not open.

Add the squid and shrimps and simmer for 1 minute. Stir in the tomatoes, season to taste with oregano, salt, and pepper, and simmer until the sauce has thickened slightly.

Drain the pasta and toss with the sauce. Sprinkle with parsley and serve at once.

ferretti al ragù di carne
handmade noodles with ragu

Despite its Italian name, you won't see any meat in this ragu. After the various meats have been stewed, they are removed to be eaten at another time as a main course. In the north of Italy, meat is boiled to make good stock for tortellini, then removed and served up as bollito misto, literally "boiled dinner."

Ferretti is a pasta made with semolina and hand-rolled into thick, spaghetti-like strips about 3 inches (8 cm) long, using a special tool called a ferretto.

Makes 8 or more servings

2 medium onions, finely chopped	2 cups/500 mL chicken stock
6 cloves garlic, chopped	1 100-oz/2.84 L can crushed tomatoes, the best quality available
½ cup/125 mL extra-virgin olive oil	
1 lb/500 g veal short ribs or brisket	salt and pepper
4 Italian sausages, of your choice	2 bunches basil, chopped
½ rack pork back ribs	2 lb/1 kg ferretti
½ cup/125 mL white wine	1 tbsp/15 mL butter
1 5.5-oz/156 mL can tomato paste	½ cup/125 mL grated provolone cheese, plus more for garnish

In a big pot over medium heat, sauté the onion and garlic in the olive oil until the vegetables are soft and translucent. Add the veal or brisket, sausages, and pork, and brown for 3–4 minutes. Pour in the wine and cook until it evaporates.

Stir in the tomato paste, mixing well, and cook for 1–2 minutes. Add the chicken stock and bring to a gentle simmer. Stir in the tomatoes, season to taste with salt and pepper, add half of the basil, and cook for at least 1½ hours at a very low simmer, stirring occasionally.

Gently remove the meat, which you can serve as a separate meal. Strain the sauce to remove the tomato seeds and other debris; it should be thick and creamy.

Cook the ferretti in plenty of boiling salted water until done to your liking. Drain the pasta and toss with the sauce. Stir in the butter, the remaining basil, and grated provolone to taste. Serve with more provolone for topping. ☙

pizzoccheri della valtellina
buckwheat fettuccine with cabbage, potato, and cheese

This dish is one of the easiest—and tastiest—to make. The cabbage, Swiss chard (silverbeet), and potato balance the coarse texture of the buckwheat. I first had buckwheat fettuccine as a young apprentice working in the Dolomite town of San Martino di Castrozza. I thought it was crazy to pair potatoes with pasta, but I soon realized I had a lot to learn about Italian cuisine!

If you don't wish to make your own pasta, use 1 lb (500 g) store-bought buckwheat fettuccine; many supermarkets, Italian food shops, and health food stores carry it.

Makes 4–6 servings

For pasta:

2½ cups/625 mL fine buckwheat flour

1 cup/250 mL all-purpose (plain) flour

For sauce:

1 large potato

3 cups/750 mL chopped Savoy cabbage

2 cups/500 mL chopped Swiss chard (silverbeet)

4 tbsp/60 mL butter

4 cloves garlic, chopped

8 sage leaves, chopped

1 cup/250 mL grated Bitto or casera cheese

To prepare the pasta, mix together the buckwheat and all-purpose (plain) flours in a large bowl. Add enough cool water to make a smooth dough; knead well. Wrap the dough in plastic wrap or cover with a bowl or damp cloth, and let sit for 15 minutes.

Use a pasta roller to make the fettuccine. Don't make the pasta too thin or too long—each strip should be about 6 inches (15 cm) long and no more than ½ inch (5 mm) wide, and just a little thicker than regular fettuccine.

Bring a pot of salted water to a boil. In the meantime, peel and slice the potato into ½-inch (5 mm) pieces. Add the potato to the water and boil for 5 minutes. Add the cabbage, Swiss chard (silverbeet), and pasta, and cook until the pasta is tender, about 2–3 minutes.

When the pasta is almost cooked, melt the butter with the garlic and sage in a large sauté pan over medium heat. Cook until the butter foams slightly.

Drain the pasta and greens and add them to the butter. Toss well, sprinkle the Bitto or casera cheese on top, toss again, and serve at once.

garganelli con le fave e prosciutto
garganelli with fava beans and crispy prosciutto

When you see fresh fava (broad) beans at the market, buy some. The delicious flavor will more than make up for the work of removing the shells and skins. Use them in salads, tossed in oil as a vegetable side dish, or simply boiled and salted as a snack. Or try them in this pasta recipe. Garganelli are small, ridged tubes of pasta. More and more supermarkets are stocking them, but if you're unable to find them, substitute penne.

Makes 4 servings

1 lb/500 g garganelli	12 slices prosciutto, finely sliced
3 tbsp/45 mL extra-virgin olive oil	2 cups/500 mL chopped and seeded fresh plum (Roma) tomatoes
2 cloves garlic, finely chopped	
1 medium onion, finely chopped	1 bunch basil
2 cups/500 mL fava (broad) beans, shelled and skinned	salt and pepper
	Parmigiano-Reggiano cheese, for garnish
1 cup/250 mL vegetable stock	

Cook the pasta in a big pot of boiling salted water. Drain, reserving about 1 cup/250 mL of the cooking water.

In the meantime, heat a saucepan over medium heat. Add 2 tbsp/30 mL of the olive oil, the garlic, and the onion, and cook until the vegetables are soft and translucent. Add the fava (broad) beans and stock; cook until the beans are tender, about 5–6 minutes.

In a skillet over low heat, heat the remaining 1 tbsp/15 mL of olive oil. Cook the prosciutto until crisp, and drain on paper towels.

Add the cooked pasta and tomatoes to the fava (broad) bean mixture and sauté over high heat for 1–2 minutes. Stir in the basil and, if it's too dry, some of the pasta cooking water. Season to taste with salt and pepper.

Serve at once, topped with the fried prosciutto and lots of Parmigiano-Reggiano.

tagliatelle all'aragosta
tagliatelle with lobster sauce

We have a tradition at Mistura: after a busy Saturday night, once all the customers have gone home and we have finished our chores, we head to the local Chinese diner and relax. Over dinner we laugh about the mistakes and misunderstandings of the night. One of the dishes we always order is fried noodles with lobster, ginger, and green onion—the inspiration for this recipe.

Makes 4 servings

1 cup/250 mL leeks, cut in half lengthwise, then in half-circles ½ inch (5 mm) thick	1 clove garlic, crushed
	½ cup/125 mL carrot, finely julienned
1 small bunch green onions	2 tbsp/30 mL white wine
2 1½-lb/625 g lobsters, or 12 oz/ 340 g frozen lobster meat, with juices	1 tbsp/15 mL grated fresh ginger
	salt and pepper
1 lb/500 g tagliatelle, fettuccine, or egg noodles	1 cup/250 mL cherry tomatoes, halved
2 tbsp/30 mL extra-virgin olive oil	2 tbsp/30 mL butter

Rinse the leeks under cold running water to remove any remaining sand; pat dry.

Chop the green onions as finely as possible; include about half of the green part.

If you are using fresh lobster, shell the lobsters and remove the tomalley (liver) and reserve. Cube the lobster meat and set aside. If you are using frozen lobster meat, retain about 4 tbsp/60 mL of the juices that come out of the meat when it thaws, to replace the tomalley.

Cook the pasta al dente in a big pot of boiling salted water, about 5–7 minutes.

In the meantime, heat the olive oil in a skillet over medium heat and sauté the leeks and garlic until soft. Add the carrot, lobster tomalley, and wine. As soon as the wine evaporates, add the lobster meat and then the ginger. Season to taste with salt and pepper.

Add the green onions and cherry tomatoes to the sauce and simmer for 1 minute. Add the cooked pasta and toss. Stir in the butter and serve at once. 🍲

couscous perlato al ragù di dentice
pearl couscous in red snapper stew

I developed this recipe at Prego della Piazza for a special dinner honoring Greek wines. I wanted to give the couscous a strong Mediterranean feel, and the result was excellent. This recipe can easily be modified for risotto or white polenta, or keep the fillet whole and serve it as a main course.

Makes 4 servings

12 oz/340 g red snapper fillet	1 cup/250mL pearl (Israeli) couscous
1 medium onion, finely chopped	sea salt and pepper
1 clove garlic, sliced	1 small bunch fresh oregano, finely chopped
2 tbsp/30 mL extra-virgin olive oil	juice of $\frac{1}{2}$ lemon
$\frac{1}{2}$ cup/125 mL white wine	zest of 1 lemon, finely grated
2 cups/500 mL tomato juice	1 hot chilli pepper, chopped
2 cups/500 mL water	

Carefully remove the skin and bones from the snapper and set the fillet aside.

In a saucepan over medium heat, sauté the onion and garlic in the olive oil until the vegetables are translucent. Add the snapper and cook gently for 3–4 minutes.

Pour in the wine and simmer until the liquid has evaporated. Pour in the tomato juice and water; simmer a few minutes. Add the couscous and simmer for 10 minutes. Season with sea salt and pepper to taste, then add the oregano, lemon juice, lemon zest, and chilli pepper.

Remove the couscous from the heat and let sit, covered, for 10 minutes. Stir to break the snapper fillet into bite-sized pieces, and serve.

gnocchi di patate e porcini
potato dumplings in porcini mushroom sauce

People who say gnocchi is boring have never tasted good gnocchi. The error most people commit when making gnocchi themselves is to overwork the dough, which results in very tough dumplings. Choosing the right potatoes is also paramount for great gnocchi—the potato flavor should be prevalent and the sauce should complement, not mask, it.

For sauce:

2 tbsp/30 mL extra-virgin olive oil

2 cloves garlic, chopped

2 cups/500 mL sliced porcini mushrooms (preferably frozen) or 1½ oz (45 g) dried, reconstituted

2 cups/500 mL seeded and finely chopped tomatoes (use canned if fresh are not available)

salt and pepper

2 bunches basil

1 bunch Italian parsley, chopped

1 tbsp/15 mL butter

For gnocchi:

2 lb/1 kg potatoes, of roughly equal size

2½ cups/550 mL all-purpose (plain) flour, plus extra for dusting

1 whole egg

2 egg yolks

½ cup/125 mL grated grana padano cheese

pinch of grated nutmeg

salt and pepper

To prepare the sauce, heat the olive oil in a sauté pan over medium heat. Sauté the garlic, and just before it turns golden, add the mushrooms and sauté until the vegetables are lightly browned. Add the tomatoes, season to taste with salt and pepper, and cook until the liquid is reduced to a creamy consistency. Reduce the heat so that it's just hot enough to keep the sauce warm until ready to serve.

In the meantime, bring the unpeeled potatoes to a boil in a large pot of salted water. Reduce the heat and simmer until the potatoes are cooked, at least 4 minutes. Drain the potatoes and lay them on a table or countertop to cool. As soon as they are cool enough to touch, peel them, then press them through a potato ricer or food mill (do not use a food processor).

Spread the riced potato on a floured wooden board and sprinkle with the flour. Add the egg and egg yolks, grana padano, nutmeg, and salt and pepper to taste. Using your hands, mix the dough gently to form a ball. Cut slices about 1 inch (2.5 cm) thick, then cut each slice into strips 1 inch (2.5 cm) thick; roll to form tube shapes. Cut each tube into 1-inch (2.5 cm) dumplings. Roll each dumpling with your thumb onto the tines of a fork, leaving a thumb indentation on one side and tine marks on the other. Continue dusting the dough with flour during this whole process.

Plunge the gnocchi into a big pot of boiling salted water. As soon as they float to the surface (about 3 minutes), remove them with a slotted spoon.

Tear the basil leaves by hand into small pieces. Add the basil, parsley, and butter to the sauce. To serve, place the gnocchi in a warmed ceramic bowl and pour the sauce on top. Toss gently.

maccheroni e peperoni
macaroni in bell pepper sauce

This recipe makes me think of gardens in the late summer, when the peppers (capsicums) are firm and shiny, succulent and sweet. The aroma of roasted peppers in the kitchen takes me down memory lane—this is the dish I prepared as a teenager for my friends after a night out. We would come back to my parents' house, being careful not to wake them up, and later laugh about the fact that I always ended up with more sauce than anyone else!

Maccheroni is the Italian name for all types of macaroni, including penne and rigatoni. Use whichever you like for this dish, or even a thick spaghetti. The sauce is too heavy, though, for a fine noodle or egg noodle.

Makes 4–6 servings

3 bell peppers (capsicums), 1 each yellow, red, and orange

1 banana pepper (capsicum), chopped

6 plum (Roma) tomatoes

1 lb/500 g macaroni (your favorite type)

½ cup/125 mL extra-virgin olive oil

2 cloves garlic, crushed

4 anchovies, chopped

1 chilli pepper, chopped

1 medium onion, finely chopped

salt and pepper

1 bunch basil, chopped

½ cup/125 mL chopped Italian parsley

grated caciocavallo cheese, for garnish

Grill the bell and banana peppers (capsicums) on a hot barbecue or under the grill in the oven, turning occasionally until the entire skin is blistered and blackened. Remove the peppers (capsicums) from the heat and place in a bowl, cover with plastic wrap, and let cool. Once the peppers (capsicums) are cool, remove the skins and seeds, and rinse gently. Cut the peppers (capsicums) into diamond shapes and set aside.

Peel the tomatoes and cut them in half, then cut each half in three lengthwise. Set aside.

Cook your favorite macaroni al dente in a big pot of boiling salted water.

In the meantime, prepare the sauce. Heat the olive oil in a saucepan over medium heat. Sauté the garlic, anchovies, and chilli pepper for 1 minute. Add the onion and cook for another 5 minutes. Add the peppers (capsicums); season with salt and pepper to taste. Stir in the tomatoes. Lower the heat and simmer for about 15 minutes, stirring often to prevent sticking and adding a bit of water if necessary.

Drain the pasta and toss with the sauce, along with the basil and parsley. Cook for 1 minute. Serve topped with grated caciocavallo.

pesce / fish

involtini di branzino al finocchio
mediterranean sea bass fillet and fennel

It's important to have a good fishmonger. Fish is highly perishable, so you need someone who not only offers good variety but also knows how to handle the fish properly. Always look for a clean store with no fishy odor. Take the time to talk to the fishmonger and get to know him or her.

When I prepare any fish I follow a few rules. The skin on large fish is usually thick and tough, so I tend to remove it. On smaller fish, if the skin is very thin, I leave it on.

Makes 4 servings

8 4-oz/115 g sea bass fillets	2 cloves garlic, crushed
4 fennel bulbs	½ tsp/1 mL crushed fennel seeds
salt and pepper	½ cup/125 mL roasted black olives, pitted
grated zest of 1 blood orange	
grated zest of 1 lemon	2 tbsp/30 mL white wine
2 tbsp/30 mL extra-virgin olive oil	½ cup/125 mL blood orange juice
	1 bunch chopped Italian parsley

Rinse the sea bass fillets under cold running water and pat dry. Carefully remove all the pin bones.

Prepare the fennel by cutting off the top of each bulb, reserving the fronds. Cut the bulbs in half, then crosswise in slices about ½ inch (5 mm) thick. Chop enough fronds to make ½ cup/125 mL.

Season the fish fillets with salt and pepper. Sprinkle with chopped fennel fronds and grated orange and lemon zest. Roll each fillet into a tight bundle and set aside.

Heat the olive oil in a frying pan. Add the garlic and fennel seeds and toast the fennel seeds for about 1 minute. Add the olives and fennel slices and sauté until a light golden color. Season to taste with salt and pepper.

Place the fish on top of the fennel, pour in the wine, and cook until the wine has evaporated. Pour in the orange juice, cover, and simmer for about 8 minutes. Adjust the seasoning to taste, stir in the parsley, and serve at once atop the remaining fennel fronds.

cozze in pentola
mussels with peas and white wine

I know this recipe is a departure from my roots, but it tastes so good, I just have to share it with you. At a restaurant that I once worked at, one of the most popular dishes on the menu was mussels in a white wine and cream sauce. Then came the 1990s, and everyone became cautious about cooking with cream. Well, I say they're all crazy! Cream is still good to cook with…in moderation, of course.

Be careful with these mollusks—you might become addicted to them.

Makes 4 servings

4 lb/2 kg fresh mussels	1 cup/250 mL green peas
1 tbsp/15 mL olive oil	½ cup/125 mL diced fresh tomatoes
1 tbsp/15 mL butter	1 sprig fresh tarragon
2 cloves garlic, crushed	¼ cup/50 mL heavy cream
salt and pepper	crusty bread, for dipping
½ cup/125 mL white wine	

Scrub the mussels in cold water with a stiff brush and pull off the beards.

Heat the olive oil and butter in a saucepan over medium-high heat. Sauté the garlic for 1 minute. Add the mussels and season with salt and pepper. Stir in the wine, peas, tomato, tarragon leaves, and cream. Cover with a lid and steam until the mussels open, 3–4 minutes. Discard any mussels that do not open.

Remove the mussels with a slotted spoon and place them in a bowl.

Reduce the liquid in the pan and add salt and pepper to taste. Pour the sauce over the mussels and serve with lots of warm crusty bread for dipping.

trancia di salmone alle olive
salmon steak with roasted black olives

I always eat salmon a little undercooked, as the flesh is creamier and very pleasant. Strong yet delicate, salmon is a favorite of many customers at the restaurant. We use it as our fallback dish on busy nights when we want to make it simple for the kitchen.

This dish goes especially well with sautéed broccoli or cauliflower.

Makes 4 servings

3 tbsp/45 mL extra-virgin olive oil	salt and pepper
2 cloves garlic, crushed	4 tbsp/60 mL white wine
4 sprigs thyme	juice of 1 lemon
8 shallots, julienned	1 tbsp/15 mL grated lemon zest
½ cup/125 mL roasted black olives, pitted	1 tbsp/15 mL butter
4 8-oz/225 g salmon steaks	

Heat the olive oil in a sauté pan over medium heat. Add the garlic, thyme, and shallots and cook for 1 minute. Add the olives and simmer gently.

Season the salmon steaks with salt and pepper and place in the pan. Turn the heat to high, sear the salmon on one side, turn it over, and add the wine, lemon juice, and lemon zest. Cover and cook for about 3 minutes. Remove from the heat and add the butter, stirring it into the sauce to incorporate. Serve at once. ☙

caciucco
seafood stew

Just about every town on the coasts of Italy has its own style of fish soup. Although at first glance they might all seem the same with their garlic and tomato, wine and bony fish, if you look closely and taste them, you'll soon realize there are subtle but obvious differences. This seafood stew is the one I learned to make in Tuscany's Versilia region. If available, use sea capon, red mullet, and conger eel instead of the monkfish, calamari, and sea bass.

Makes 4 servings

4 tbsp/60 mL extra-virgin olive oil

4 cloves garlic, chopped

1 medium onion, chopped

2 bay leaves

1 bunch thyme

12 littleneck clams in their shells, scrubbed and rinsed

½ cup/125 mL white wine

2 cups/500 mL chopped fresh plum (Roma) tomatoes

1 cup/250 mL chicken stock

1 chilli pepper, chopped

salt and pepper

8 oz/225 g monkfish tail, cut in 4 pieces

8 oz/225 g calamari, cut in short strips

8 oz/225 g sea bass or 2 fillets, cut in half

4 jumbo shrimps

16 mussels in their shells, scrubbed and rinsed

1 lemon

4 slices crusty bread

crushed garlic

olive oil, for garnish

Heat the olive oil in a heavy-bottomed pot over high heat. Sauté the garlic, onion, bay leaves, and thyme for 1 minute. Place the clams in the pot and pour in the wine. Cover the pot and cook the clams for a few minutes, until they open. Discard any that do not open.

Add the tomatoes, chicken stock, and chilli pepper. Season to taste with salt and pepper and simmer for 1 minute. Gently place the monkfish tail in the pot, followed by the calamari, sea bream, shrimps, and mussels. Simmer gently for about 8 minutes. Taste and adjust the seasoning. Squeeze the juice of the lemon over top.

Rub the bread slices with crushed garlic, then grill them. Spoon the stew onto the garlic toast, sprinkle olive oil on top, and enjoy. 🍲

gamberi e fagioli
sweet shrimp and cannellini beans

In the fall, just after watering season, the irrigation canals in Italy are abundant with sweet shrimp, crawfish, and smelt. Anyone can catch them easily with nothing more than a homemade net. Osterie throughout the region fry up their daily catch: a bowl of shrimp and beans with a glass of wine—you can't go wrong with that. I like to keep the shells on the shrimp for this dish, but feel free to remove them if you prefer.

Makes 4 servings

3 tbsp/45 mL extra-virgin olive oil	1½ cups/375 mL cannellini beans
2 shallots, finely minced	½ cup/125 mL chopped roasted red peppers (capsicums)
1 tsp/5 mL fennel seeds, crushed	
2 lb/1 kg pink shrimp	salt and pepper
½ cup/125 mL white wine	2 tbsp/30 mL chopped fresh chervil
1 tbsp/15 mL white wine vinegar	

Heat the olive oil in a sauté pan over medium heat. Add the shallots and fennel seeds and cook for 1 minute. Add the shrimps, wine, and vinegar; cook for 1–2 minutes.

Stir in the beans and red peppers (capsicums) and season to taste with salt and pepper. As soon as the shrimp and beans begin to sauté, cover and cook for 2 minutes. Stir in the chervil, adjust the seasoning to taste, and serve at once. ☕

capesante con pancetta
roasted sea scallops with bacon

When buying scallops, make sure they are fresh and have not been chemically treated—befriending your fishmonger can be very beneficial! Scallops are quick and versatile to cook. They are great in pasta, as an appetizer or main course, marinated raw or cooked, fried, sautéed, or baked. Just remember, the longer you cook them, the tougher they will be.

Makes 4 servings

16 large sea scallops	2 shallots, finely chopped
16 slices flat pancetta	1 tbsp/15 mL capers
2 tbsp/30 mL extra-virgin olive oil	1 tbsp/15 mL balsamic vinegar
1 tbsp/15 mL butter	½ cup/125 mL red wine
1 clove garlic, lightly crushed	

Rinse the scallops and pat dry. Wrap each scallop with a slice of pancetta, leaving the top and bottom exposed.

Heat the olive oil in a heavy-bottomed pan over medium-high heat. Add the butter and the scallops, searing them until golden on the bottom. Flip the scallops and add the garlic and shallots to the pan. Cook the scallops for another minute.

Add the capers and balsamic vinegar, cooking until the vinegar has evaporated. Pour in the wine and cook for another 2 minutes. Serve at once.

storione in agrodolce
sturgeon fillet in red wine vinegar sauce

As a boy I would go fishing for sturgeon with my uncle on Italy's great Po River. Although the fishing was highly regulated, we still managed to get at least one for ourselves and some to sell.

Sturgeon is a prehistoric-looking fish; its texture is firm and similar to swordfish when cooked. Swordfish or any other firm white fish would work in this recipe.

Makes 4 servings

2 tbsp/30 mL vegetable oil	2 tbsp/30 mL red wine vinegar
2 cups/500 mL cipolline (Italian pearl onions)	4 tbsp/60 mL tomato sauce
salt and pepper	4 8-oz/225 g sturgeon steaks, each 1 inch (2.5 cm) thick
2 tbsp/30 mL sugar	2 tbsp/30 mL Italian parsley, chopped

Heat the vegetable oil in a sauté pan over medium heat. Add the cipolline, season to taste with salt and pepper, add the sugar, and cook gently until the cipolline are golden. Sprinkle the vinegar over the cipolline and cook 1–2 minutes to allow some of the vinegar's acidity to evaporate. Stir in the tomato sauce and cook until the cipolline are soft. If the pan is too dry, add a bit of water.

Rinse the sturgeon steaks under cold running water and pat dry. Place the steaks in the pan so they are surrounded by the cipolline but not covering them. Cook, covered, for about 6 minutes, shaking the pan occasionally to prevent sticking. Add the parsley and serve at once.

halibut ai funghi
halibut and chanterelle mushrooms

Halibut, a fish from the North Atlantic, was almost unknown in Italy until recently. There it's known by its English name, as very few people know its name in Italian: ippoglosso (truth be told, I had to look it up myself). Bright white, meaty, and delicate, halibut lends itself to many styles of preparation. If halibut is not available, use swordfish or any firm white fish.

Makes 4 servings

2 tbsp/30 mL light olive oil	1 tbsp/15 mL chopped fresh tarragon
4 8-oz/225 g halibut steaks	4 tbsp/60 mL white wine
salt and pepper	6 tbsp/90 mL heavy cream
1½ cups/375 mL sliced leeks, white part only	1 tbsp/15 mL butter
1½ cups/375 mL chanterelle mushrooms, cleaned, large ones halved	1 tbsp/15 mL chopped chervil
1 cup/250 mL grape tomatoes, halved	

Heat the olive oil in a heavy-bottomed pan over high heat. Season the halibut with salt and pepper and sear until slightly golden. Transfer to a plate.

Add the leeks and chanterelle mushrooms to the pan and sauté gently until the vegetables are wilted. Add the tomatoes and tarragon, then return the fish to the pan to sear the other side.

Pour in the wine and cook until it has evaporated. Pour in the cream; cover the pan to cook for about 6 minutes. Transfer the fish to a plate.

Add the butter and chervil to the sauce, stir, and adjust the seasoning to taste. Cook until the liquid is reduced to the desired consistency, about 1 minute or less. Drizzle the sauce over the fish and serve at once.

ragù di moscardini
sautéed baby octopus

My first real restaurant job was in 1975, at Trattoria dall'Amelia in Mestre, near Venice. One day, Chef shouted for me. "Clean this," he ordered. Being from the center of northern Italy, I had never seen an octopus before, let alone cleaned one. It took some time to get the hang of it, but was it ever worth it! Chef let me try some of the cooked octopus, and the flavor and texture were fantastic. It's a taste experience I've never forgotten.

If cooked properly, these tiny octopus will be crunchy but not tough. They're particularly good served over slices of grilled polenta. Sometimes I also add a few fresh or frozen peas in the last few minutes of cooking.

Makes 4 servings

½ cup/50 mL extra-virgin olive oil	2 tbsp/30 mL tomato paste
2 lb/1 kg tiny octopus, blanched	2 cups/500 mL fresh plum (Roma) tomatoes, peeled, seeded, and chopped
1 medium onion, chopped	
4 cloves garlic, chopped	salt and pepper
1 cup/250 mL white wine	

Heat the olive oil in a medium saucepan. Add the octopus and sauté until the flesh wrinkles, about 2 minutes. Some browning isn't a problem.

Add the onion and garlic, stirring to prevent burning. Add the wine and cook until it evaporates. Stir in the tomato paste and cook until dry, about 3–5 minutes. Add the tomatoes, season to taste, and simmer for 15–25 minutes, or until the octopus is fork-tender.

seppie al nero
squid stewed in its own sauce

I first tried this dish at Trattoria dall'Amelia, where I worked as a teenager. Among all the new things I was experiencing, this was the strangest. Don't let the squid's appearance turn you off—you'll be amazed at how good it tastes. Serve with polenta or a risotto, or on spaghetti.

Makes 4 servings

2 lb/1 kg squid	½ cup/125 mL finely chopped onion
3 tbsp/45 mL extra-virgin olive oil	1 chilli pepper, chopped
2 cloves garlic, finely chopped	½ cup/125 mL white wine

Clean the squid, retaining the ink sacs. Cut the squid tubes in half, then into 2-inch (5 cm) strips. Wash well and pat dry with paper towels.

Heat the olive oil in a sauté pan over medium heat. Add the garlic, onion, and chilli pepper and cook for about 1 minute. Add the squid and sauté for a few minutes, stirring well.

Over a bowl, squeeze the ink sacs to extract the ink. Stir in the wine. Strain and pour the liquid over the squid in the pan. Season to taste with salt and pepper, and cook over high heat for about 5 minutes, until the sauce is black and reduced. Serve at once.

pollame / poultry

pollo alla fiorentina
florentine fried chicken

A colleague back in Italy had the task of roasting chicken for the hotel staff twice a week. He put great effort into it, making the skin perfectly crisp and golden. He loved chicken so much that his dream was to move to America and open a restaurant-farm where he would raise, cook, and serve chicken, fried, roasted, and grilled. When I arrived in North America, I called to give him the bad news: everybody makes chicken that way here, even the chain restaurants. But move over, Southern-style fried chicken—it's time to taste the original!

Note: Dried herbs can be a substituted for fresh, but use fresh if available.

Makes 4–6 servings

4 bay leaves	3 eggs
2 cloves garlic	2 tbsp/30 mL chopped Italian parsley
1 sprig thyme	salt and pepper
1 sprig rosemary	2 cups/500 mL all-purpose (plain) flour
1 sprig sage	
juice of 2 lemons	4 cups/1 L grapeseed oil, light olive oil, or other light oil
1 yellow-skinned grain-fed chicken, weighing 2–3 lb/1–1.5 kg	

With a mortar and pestle, crush the bay leaves, garlic, thyme, rosemary, and sage to extract the flavor. Add the lemon juice, then pour the mixture into a clean plastic bag.

Quarter the chicken, remove most of the bones, and cut each quarter in half (or ask your butcher to do this). Rinse and pat dry. Put the chicken in the plastic bag with the herbs and lemon juice and refrigerate for 2–3 hours.

Beat the eggs in a bowl, add the parsley, and season with salt and pepper. Remove the chicken from the bag and dredge each piece with flour, coating well and shaking off any excess. Dip each chicken piece into the egg mixture to coat well. Dredge again with the flour.

Fry the chicken in the oil at 275°F (140°C) until golden-crisp; the oil should not be too hot or it will burn the chicken skin before it cooks the meat.

Season the chicken with salt and pepper, and enjoy. ☺

fagiano all'uva
roasted pheasant with green grapes

When the yearly hunting season in Italy opens, the riversides are teeming with hunters looking for hares and pheasants. My uncle used to take me along. Needless to say, I didn't catch much, but my uncle was a seasoned hunter and he always brought home a variety of game.

Makes 4 servings

1 cup/250 mL seedless green grapes	1 cup/250 mL diced pancetta
½ cup/125 mL white wine	1 tbsp/15 mL wildflower honey
4 8-oz/225 g pheasant breasts, skin on	2 tbsp/30 mL verjuice or 1 tbsp/ 15 mL white wine vinegar
salt and pepper	2 cups/500 mL seedless grapes (red, green, and black in equal amounts)
2 tbsp/30 mL extra-virgin olive oil	
4 shallots, finely minced	1 tbsp/15 mL butter

Puree the 1 cup/250 mL of green grapes and ¼ cup/50 mL of the wine in a blender. Pass through a fine mesh strainer and set aside.

Season the pheasant breasts with salt and pepper. Heat the oil in a skillet over medium-high heat. Cook the pheasant, skin side down, until golden, about 4 minutes. Turn the pheasant over, add the shallots and pancetta, and cook for 2 minutes. Sprinkle on the remaining ¼ cup/50 mL wine and cook until it evaporates.

Add the grape/wine juice, honey, and verjuice or vinegar; cook for about 5 minutes over low heat. Increase the heat to medium, add the grapes, and simmer, covered, for about 5 minutes.

Transfer the pheasant to a plate and cover with tinfoil. In the meantime, reduce the sauce by about half, until it has a creamy consistency. This might take 5 or more minutes, depending on how liquid the sauce is at this point. Season to taste with salt and pepper, add the butter, and return the pheasant to the pan to reheat.

pollo alla cacciatora
chicken cacciatora

All cooks need to have a fallback traditional recipe in their repertoire—let this be it! This easy dish is one of the first I was allowed to cook on my own. For a simple meal, serve it with grilled polenta, buttered noodles, steamed rice, or mashed potatoes. Substitute porcini or chanterelle mushrooms for champignons, and you've changed the class of this dish—you will make a bella figura (good impression).

Makes 4 servings

8 chicken legs	½ cup/125 mL white wine
salt and pepper	2 red bell peppers (capsicums), cut into wedges
4 tbsp/60 mL extra-virgin olive oil	
6 cloves garlic, finely chopped	2 cups/500 mL white champignon mushrooms, quartered
1 medium onion, finely chopped	
2 stalks celery, finely chopped	1 cup/250 mL plum (Roma) tomatoes, seeded and diced
1 medium carrot, finely chopped	½ cup/125 mL chicken stock
2 bay leaves	½ bunch Italian parsley, chopped

Season the chicken legs with salt and pepper. Heat the oil in a heavy-bottomed pot over high heat. Sear the chicken legs, until golden; turn over and sear the other side. Add the garlic, onion, celery, carrot, and bay leaves to the pot; stir and let cook for about 4 minutes. Pour in the wine and cook until it evaporates.

Add the peppers (capsicums), mushrooms, tomatoes, and stock and stir well. Reduce the heat to low and simmer, covered, for about 20–30 minutes.

When the chicken is cooked, transfer it to a plate and let it sit, covered, for 10 minutes. Reduce the sauce to a creamy consistency, adjust the seasoning, and stir in the parsley. Return the chicken to the pot to reheat and serve with the sauce spooned over top. 🍲

galletto alle spèzie
spiced cornish game hen

From the time we started developing this recipe at the restaurant, we knew it was going to be a hit. The Asian spices are not overpowering, but complement the game hen. Perfect served with spinach, Brussels sprouts, bok choy, or broccoli.

Note: Use pre-ground spices or grind them yourself in a spice grinder or coffee mill.

Makes 4 servings

For marinade:	For game hens:
½ tsp/2 mL ground fennel seeds	2 Cornish game hens
½ tsp/2 mL ground coriander seeds	2 tbsp/30 mL vegetable oil
½ tsp/2 mL ground star anise	2 tbsp/30 mL butter
½ tsp/2 mL paprika	4 cloves garlic, crushed
½ tsp/2 mL ground cardamom seeds	1 sprig fresh sage
1 tsp/5 mL sugar	1 sprig rosemary
2 tbsp/30 mL vegetable oil	1 bay leaf
	salt and pepper
	2 cups/500 mL cubed boiled potatoes

Preheat the oven to 450°F (230°C).

Combine all the marinade ingredients in a small bowl. Split the Cornish game hens in half at the backbone, brush on the marinade, and marinate for at least 1–2 hours.

Heat the oil and butter in a roasting pan over medium heat. Place the marinated game hens, skin side down, in the pan and cook on top of the stove for about 10 minutes. Turn the hens over, add the garlic, herbs, salt and pepper, and potatoes, and bake in the oven for about 10 minutes, reducing the heat to 400°F (200°C) if the meat and potatoes start to brown too much.

Turn the oven off and open the door, keeping it ajar. Let the meat sit for 10 more minutes in the oven. Remove from the oven and gently remove the ribs and hip bones from the hens.

To serve, scoop the potatoes into the center of individual serving plates, along with your choice of vegetables, and place a hen half on top of each.

involtino di pollo alle melanzane
chicken rolls with eggplant

When you're feeling a little playful in the kitchen, try this recipe.
Involtini—stuffed rolls of meat or fish—were very popular when I was
growing up in Italy, and one never knew what they would be stuffed with.
Experiment with the many possible combinations—turkey, pork, veal,
beef. Fish is also a great choice for lighter meals.

Makes 4 servings

2 long (Japanese if available) eggplants	1 clove garlic, minced
	2 tbsp/30 mL finely chopped onion
4 large boneless, skinless chicken breasts	2 tbsp/30 mL capers
	1 sprig thyme
pepper	4 tbsp/60 mL white wine
extra-virgin olive oil, for dressing the eggplant	2 tbsp/30 mL chopped plum (Roma) tomatoes
1 lb/500 g smoked scamorza cheese	1 bunch Italian parsley, finely chopped
1 tbsp/15 mL extra-virgin olive oil	
1 tbsp/15 mL butter	

Cut the eggplants lengthwise into ½-inch (5 mm) slices. Salt and set
aside to drain for up to 30 minutes, to remove bitterness.

Slice each chicken breast at a 45-degree angle into four slices. Flatten
the slices with a meat mallet to an even thickness.

Dry the eggplant and season with pepper and olive oil. Grill lightly—they
shouldn't be too brown. Trim the ends so they are the same length as
the chicken slices.

Place a slice of eggplant on a slice of chicken breast and top with a slice of scamorza; roll up the meat. Repeat this procedure with the remaining chicken breast slices. Align four rolls and skewer them with two bamboo sticks long enough to just penetrate the meat, to keep the rolls from unraveling.

Heat the olive oil and butter in a medium skillet over medium-high heat. Sear the skewered rolls on both sides until golden. Add the garlic and onion, and cook for 2–3 minutes, until soft and translucent.

Stir in the capers and thyme leaves. Pour in the wine and cook until it evaporates. Add the tomato and simmer, covered, for 10 minutes. Sprinkle in the parsley, then transfer the chicken to individual serving plates or a serving platter.

Remove the bamboo sticks, spoon the sauce over top, and serve.

petto d'anatra con funghi chiodini
duck breast with mushrooms

Growing up on a farm is a great way to start a culinary life. My parents always had plenty of ducks and on occasion one would end up in a pot. This is a modern version of a duck stew we typically ate in the autumn, when mushrooms are plentiful.

Makes 4 servings

4 boneless young duck breasts, each weighing 8–12 oz/225–340 g	1 cup/250 mL honey mushrooms, separated, or your favorite mushroom, sliced
salt and pepper	2 cups/500 mL grape tomatoes, cut in half
4 tbsp/60 mL sherry	
1 tbsp/15 mL red wine vinegar	½ cup/125 mL chicken stock
4 cloves garlic, peeled and chopped	1 bunch Italian parsley, chopped

Rinse the duck breasts under cold running water and pat dry with paper towels. Score the skin lightly and season with salt and pepper.

Heat a large skillet over medium-high heat and cook them, skin side down, until the skin is crisp and the meat has released its fat, about 5–10 minutes.

Remove most of the fat from the skillet, reserving a spoonful, and turn the duck breasts over. Sprinkle with the sherry and vinegar and cook until the liquid evaporates. Remove the duck wrap in tinfoil, and set aside.

To the same skillet add the reserved duck fat and the garlic. Just before the garlic turns brown, add the mushrooms and season with salt and pepper. Add the tomatoes and sauté for 2–3 minutes.

Add the chicken stock and return the duck breasts to the pan. Increase the heat to high and cook the sauce for a few minutes, until it is reduced to the desired consistency. Stir in the parsley and serve.

petto di tacchino ai carciofi
turkey cutlets with minted artichokes

Turkey is not only for the holidays—it's delicious anytime, and cooking turkey cutlets is fast and easy. And don't be afraid of fresh artichokes. Choose artichokes with tight heads that feel heavy and are green or gray-green in color.

Makes 4 servings

juice of 1 lemon

12 small fresh globe artichokes

2 lb/1 kg boneless turkey breast, cut into 8 cutlets of equal size

salt and pepper

1 tbsp/15 mL butter

1 tbsp/15 mL extra-virgin olive oil

2 cloves garlic, crushed

1 medium white onion, finely chopped

½ cup/50 mL white wine

grated zest of 2 lemons

½ cup/50 mL chicken stock, plus more as needed

2 tbsp/30 mL finely chopped Italian parsley

2 tbsp/30 mL chopped mint

Add the lemon juice to a bowl of cold water to acidulate the water. To prepare the artichokes, cut off the top quarter and discard. Remove the tough outer leaves by bending them back and snapping them off at the base. Peel the stem, if necessary. Cut the artichokes in half and remove the fuzzy centers, or chokes (small artichokes shouldn't have much of a center). Cut the artichokes into thin wedges, immediately submerging them in the acidulated cold water as you do so, to prevent discoloring.

With a meat mallet, pound the turkey breasts to ½ inch (2 cm) thick. Season with salt and pepper. Heat the butter and olive oil in a sauté pan over medium-high heat, and sear the turkey cutlets until lightly golden on one side.

Add the garlic and onion and cook for 2 minutes. Add the artichokes, wine, and lemon zest, then turn the cutlets over to cook on the other side. Once the wine has evaporated, add the chicken stock. Cook for another 2 minutes, adding more stock if the pan becomes too dry.

Transfer the turkey to a serving plate. Add the parsley and mint to the sauté pan, stirring to incorporate them, and simmer to reduce the sauce to a creamy consistency. Adjust the seasoning to taste, spoon the sauce over the cutlets, and serve.

carne / meat

fegato alla veneziana
venetian liver and onions

If you love liver, this recipe just might become one of your favorites. The thin slices of liver and the sweetness of the onion go hand in hand. Enjoy this dish with polenta or mashed potatoes.

Makes 4 servings

1 lb/500 g calf's liver	3 cups/750 mL thinly sliced sweet white onion
salt and pepper	½ cup/125 mL white wine
2 tbsp/30 mL extra-virgin olive oil, plus more for seasoning	½ cup/125 mL Italian parsley
2 tbsp/30 mL butter	½ lemon

Trim the hard sinew and outer membrane from the liver, being careful not to crush it. Slice the liver into scaloppine about 2 inches (5 cm) wide and ½ inch (1 cm) thick; season with olive oil, salt, and pepper.

Heat 2 tbsp/30 mL of olive oil and the butter in a skillet over medium-low heat. Gently sauté the onion until it is caramelized. Turn the heat to high and immediately add the liver. Sear on both sides. Pour in the wine and cook until it evaporates. Season to taste with salt and pepper, parsley, and a squeeze of lemon juice, and stir well. Serve at once.

manzo brasato aromatico
braised short ribs in red wine

Maybe it's because I grew up in the interior of northern Italy, where good fish is not as plentiful as elsewhere in the country, but I am very comfortable cooking meats. Whether they're boiled, stewed, or thinly sliced and grilled with Asian seasonings, short ribs are one cut of meat I'm particularly fond of. This recipe is wonderful accompanied by lightly sautéed bok choy, spinach, or potatoes.

Makes 4–6 servings

1 sprig each rosemary, thyme, and sage	salt and pepper
1 tsp/5 mL fresh ginger, chopped	3 cloves garlic, crushed
3 star anise	1½ cups/375 mL diced onion
3 bay leaves	1 cup/250 mL diced carrots
2 tbsp/30 mL extra-virgin olive oil	½ cup/125 mL diced celery
1 tsp/5 mL butter	4 tbsp/60 mL tomato paste
4 lb/2 kg beef chuck short ribs, frenched (ask your butcher)	1 cup/250 mL red wine
	3 cups/750 mL unsalted beef stock

To prepare the herb sachet, place the rosemary, thyme, sage, ginger, star anise, and bay leaves onto a 4x4-inch (10x10 cm) square of cheesecloth, gather the cloth into a bundle, and tie it up with twine.

Heat the oil and butter in a heavy-bottomed pot over medium-high heat. Season the short ribs with salt and pepper and sear until the meat is golden brown. Add the garlic, onion, carrot, and celery, and stir until the vegetables are translucent. Stir in the tomato paste and cook for 2–3 minutes. Add the herb sachet.

Pour in the red wine and boil until it evaporates. Pour in the stock, reduce the heat to low, and simmer, covered, for at least 2½ hours, or until the meat is fork-tender. Remove the meat from the pot, wrap in tinfoil, and set aside.

Reduce the sauce to a creamy consistency, strain out all the vegetables, and season to taste with salt and pepper. Return the meat to the pot with the sauce and reheat to serve.

costine di maiale e verze
pork spareribs and cabbage

Spareribs are a favorite for summer barbecues. This recipe captures the style of the ribs I ate growing up—few things work as well together as pork and cabbage. This hearty dish is especially good in winter, served with potato salad or grilled polenta.

Makes 4 servings

4 whole racks baby back ribs	2 tbsp/30 mL red wine vinegar
salt and pepper	1 tbsp/15 mL tomato paste
1 tbsp/15 mL sugar	1 cup/250 mL chopped fresh tomatoes
3 tbsp/45 mL extra-virgin olive oil	
2 cloves garlic, crushed	1 cup/250 mL chicken stock
1 cup/250 mL julienned onion	1 head cabbage, hard outer leaves removed
½ cup/125 mL white wine	

Wash the ribs and pat dry. Cut between each bone to separate them, and season with salt, pepper, and sugar.

Heat the olive oil in a heavy-bottomed pot over medium-high heat. Add the ribs and sear until golden brown. Add the garlic and onion and cook for a few minutes. Pour in the wine and vinegar and cook until they evaporate. Stir in the tomato paste and then the tomatoes. Pour in the chicken stock, reduce the heat, and simmer for about 20 minutes, covered.

In the meantime, remove each leaf from the cabbage and cut out the center spine, splitting the leaf in two. Cut the cabbage into wide juliennes. Add the cabbage to the meat, season with salt and pepper, stir, and cover. Simmer until the cabbage is tender, about 10 minutes.

coda di bue al barolo
barolo-braised oxtail

When I was growing up in Italy, my mother often prepared oxtail, as it was an affordable meat. Back in those days we thought of braising—which requires robust cuts of meat—as a bad thing. How things have changed! Today braised meats have achieved gourmet status. This dish is excellent with mashed potatoes or polenta of any type, or break the meat down, remove the bones, and use it for pasta, gnocchi, or risotto. A good wine will enhance the flavor of this dish, so don't skimp.

Makes 4 servings

1 sprig each rosemary, sage, thyme, and parsley, for sachet (or ½ tsp/ 2 mL of each if using dried herbs)

2 tbsp/30 mL extra-virgin olive oil

1 tbsp/15 mL butter

4 lb/2 kg oxtail

salt and pepper

4 cloves garlic

1 cup/250 mL diced onion

1 cup/250 mL diced celery

1 cup/250 mL diced carrots

1 cup/250 mL peeled, diced parsnips

4 bay leaves

4 tbsp/60 mL tomato paste

2 cups/500 mL Barolo wine

4 cups/1 L unsalted beef stock

To prepare the fresh herb sachet, place the herbs on a 4x4-inch (10 x10 cm) square of cheesecloth, gather the cloth into a bundle, and tie it up with twine. (If you are using dried herbs, they can simply be added loose.)

Heat the oil and the butter in a heavy-bottomed pot over medium-high heat. Season the oxtail with salt and pepper and sear until golden brown on all sides. Add the garlic, onion, celery, carrots, parsnip, and bay leaves, and stir until the vegetables are translucent. Stir in the tomato paste and cook for a few minutes. Toss in the herbs.

Pour in the wine and boil until it evaporates. Pour in the beef stock and simmer over low heat, covered, for at least 1½ hours; when the meat falls off the bone easily, it's done. Transfer the meat to a plate and cover. Allow it to cool completely before touching it again.

Pass the vegetables through a food mill or blend in a food processor and return to the pot with the juices. Reduce the sauce to the desired thickness and season to taste with salt and pepper. Return the meat to the pot and reheat to serve.

coniglio in umido
rabbit in apricot sauce

Rabbit is a very popular meat in Italy and, being low in fat, one of the healthiest. My parents used to keep rabbits by the hundreds. We sold them, and on occasion one would end up in a pot—delicious!

Note: Marinate the apricots in the grappa 8–12 hours ahead of time.

Makes 4–6 servings

1 cup/250 mL dried apricots, halved

4 tbsp/60 mL grappa di moscato

2 small rabbits, approximately 3 lb/ 1.5 kg each, deboned and cut into large pieces (ask your butcher)

salt and pepper

4 tbsp/60 mL vegetable oil

16 shallots, sliced

3 star anise

2 bay leaves

½ cup/125 mL white wine

2 tbsp/30 mL tomato paste

4 plum (Roma) tomatoes, peeled, seeded, and quartered

2 cups/500 mL chicken stock

1 tsp/5 mL chopped chives

2 tbsp/30 mL chopped fresh sorrel

Marinate the dried apricots in the grappa (see note).

Season the rabbit pieces with salt and pepper. Heat the oil in a sauté pan and cook the rabbit until golden. Stir in the shallots and grappa-soaked apricots and cook for 1 minute. Add the star anise, bay leaves, and wine; cook until the wine evaporates. Stir in the tomato paste and cook for 2–3 minutes.

Add the tomatoes and chicken stock and simmer gently, covered, for at least 1 hour. Test a rabbit leg for doneness by pressing gently on the thickest part—the meat should give and break apart easily. Remove the rabbit and set aside, covered with tinfoil.

Reduce the pan juices to a creamy consistency, season to taste with salt and pepper, and add the chives and sorrel, stirring to mix well. Return the rabbit to the pan with any juices it may have purged while cooling, to reheat.

To serve, arrange the rabbit pieces on a plate with the shallots, apricots, and tomatoes around them and the sauce poured over top.

costine di agnello glassate al balsamico
balsamic-glazed lamb ribs

If you are lucky enough to find lamb ribs, grab them and run home to try this recipe.

This dish has become so popular at Mistura that I can't even suggest taking it off the menu without creating an uproar.

Makes 4 servings

2 tbsp/30 mL extra-virgin olive oil	1 cup/250 mL red wine
4 lb/2 kg lamb ribs	2 cups/500 mL chicken stock
salt and pepper	½ cup/125 mL tomato paste
5 cloves garlic, crushed	tzatziki sauce, for serving
2 onions, diced	
2 carrots, diced	**For glaze:**
1 stalk celery, diced	1 cup/250 mL balsamic vinegar
8 sprigs rosemary	¼ cup/75 mL maple syrup
8 sprigs thyme	2 tbsp/30 mL tomato paste
2 bay leaves	

Heat 1 tbsp/15 mL olive oil in a large skillet or casserole dish over medium-high heat. Season the ribs with salt and pepper and sear in batches until browned on both sides. Remove from the pan and set aside.

Lower the heat to medium and add the remaining 1 tbsp/15 mL oil. Sauté the garlic, onion, carrots, celery, rosemary, thyme, and bay leaves until the vegetables are soft and golden brown, about 5 minutes. Add the wine and cook until it evaporates. Return the lamb to the pan and add the chicken stock and tomato paste. Cover and cook for 1½ hours, or until the lamb is tender. Remove the lamb from the pan and keep warm.

Preheat the oven to 350°F (180°C).

To prepare the glaze, strain the pan juices into a bowl, discarding any solids. Pour into a sauté pan along with the balsamic vinegar, maple syrup, and tomato paste. Bring to a boil and cook until thick and syrupy. Brush the glaze over the ribs and reheat in the oven for 10 minutes, or until heated through. Serve with tzatziki sauce on the side.

braciola di maiale con salvia e limone
pan-seared pork chops with lemon sage

The sweet aroma of pan-fried pork chops is mouth-watering, and the meat marries naturally with sage and lemon. The acidity of the lemon cuts the fat and freshens the flavor—the main reason why Italian dishes, from grilled meat to fish to pasta, are often served with fresh lemon. Just remember, a drop of lemon juice goes a long way.

If you are considering leaving out the cream, don't. Even though it is only a small amount, it imparts a flavor that completes the dish.

Makes 4 servings

2 lemons	1 tbsp/15 mL butter
4 pork chops	1 bunch sage
all-purpose (plain) flour, for dredging	4 shallots, finely minced
salt and pepper	½ tsp/2 mL Dijon mustard
1 tsp/5 mL vegetable oil	2 tbsp/30 mL heavy cream

Zest the lemons. Peel and separate one of them into segments. Juice the second lemon.

Lightly dredge the pork chops with flour seasoned with salt and pepper. Heat the vegetable oil and 1 tsp/5 mL butter in a skillet over medium-high heat. Add the chops and sear on both sides until golden. Transfer to a plate.

Melt the remaining 2 tsp/10 mL butter in the pan. Add the sage leaves and cook until they release an aroma. Add the shallots and cook for 1 minute. Add the lemon zest, return the chops to the pan, and sprinkle them with the lemon juice. Stir in the lemon segments and Dijon mustard and cook for a few minutes.

Pour in the cream and simmer until the pork chops are cooked and the sauce is well reduced. Season to taste with salt and pepper.

crocchette di rosa
rosa's veal-and-rice croquettes

Working in a restaurant means I'm often busy six or seven days a week. Fortunately, my wife, Rosa, has the strength to rise to the challenge. She has quite a few recipes in her arsenal, and this one is a favorite. When I come home late at night, often after midnight, it's a welcome surprise to find a plate of these croquettes waiting for me on the table. Rosa has learned, though, not to leave too many—for my own good!

Makes 4–6 servings

For croquettes:

4 cups/1 L cooked risotto or leftover rice

2 cups/500 mL lean ground veal

2 eggs

½ cup/125 mL grated Parmigiano-Reggiano cheese

½ cup/125 mL Italian parsley, chopped

1 tbsp/15 mL extra-virgin olive oil

1 tbsp/15 mL butter

2 cloves garlic, chopped

½ cup/150 mL finely diced onion

½ cup/150 mL finely diced celery

½ cup/150 mL finely diced carrot

1 cup/250 mL green peas

salt and pepper

For breading:

2 eggs

1 cup/250 mL milk

2 tbsp/30 mL grated Parmigiano-Reggiano cheese

salt and pepper

2–3 cups/500–750 mL breadcrumbs, as needed

light olive oil, for frying

In a mixing bowl, combine the rice, ground veal, eggs, Parmigiano, and parsley.

Heat the oil and butter in a skillet over medium heat and sauté the garlic, onion, celery, carrot, and peas until the vegetables are translucent.

Add the vegetables to the rice and meat, mixing well. Using your hands, form into log-shaped croquettes 2½ inches (6 cm) long and 1 inch (2.5 cm) thick. Pack them well so that they will not fall apart during cooking.

To prepare the breading, beat the eggs with the milk and Parmigiano; season with salt and pepper. Spread the breadcrumbs on a plate or tray. Gently dip the croquettes in the egg wash, then roll in the breadcrumbs.

Pan-fry the croquettes in light olive oil or bake at 375°F (190°C), turning occasionally, until they are crisp and the veal is well cooked, at least 10 minutes.

legumi / vegetables

finocchi alla milanese
milanese fennel cutlets

I have yet to meet anybody who doesn't enjoy breaded meat, fish, or vegetables. Perhaps it's the richness of the frying that makes us like them so much. But I have a different take on it—if you use the right ingredients and treat them with respect, the result will be hard to resist. To me, fennel tastes so good that frying it is merely the final step in preparing a great little treat. If the frying oil is kept hot, the fennel won't be greasy.

Makes 4–6 servings

2 fennel bulbs	salt and pepper
2 eggs	3 cups/750 mL fresh breadcrumbs
½ cup/125 mL milk	½ cup/125 mL grated grana padano cheese
2 tbsp/30 mL Italian parsley, finely chopped	extra-virgin olive oil, for frying
1 tsp/5 mL fresh thyme	1 tbsp/15 mL butter

Bring a pot of salted water to a boil. Remove the stringy inedible outer leaf from each fennel bulb, clean the bottom, and cut the bulb lengthwise into wedges. Plunge the fennel into the boiling water for 30 seconds. Drain and cool on paper towels.

In a bowl, combine the eggs, milk, parsley, and thyme; season to taste with salt and pepper. Add the fennel wedges and gently stir to coat.

On a tray, mix together the breadcrumbs and the grana padano. Coat each fennel wedge by pressing it firmly into the breadcrumb mixture, being careful not to crush the fennel by pressing too hard.

In a frying pan over medium-high heat, pour olive oil to about ½ inch (5 mm) deep—there should be just enough so the fennel won't burn to the bottom of the pan, but it shouldn't be submerged in the oil—and add the butter. When it has melted, arrange the fennel wedges so they fit comfortably in the pan; they should be neither too tight against each other nor too loose. Fry the fennel until golden, turning as necessary so that it colors evenly. Remove from the oil with a slotted spoon and drain on paper towels. Serve hot or at room temperature.

cardi al forno con pecorino
baked cardoons with pecorino

The cardoon, a sweet vegetable resembling white celery, is a close cousin of the artichoke. Although cardoons (young Scotch thistles) can be relatively difficult to find, they're well worth seeking out. Like artichokes, they must be handled with care, as they tend to discolor quickly. In many locales the best season for cardoons is winter.

Makes 4–6 servings

2 bunches cardoons	2 tbsp/30 mL Italian parsley
4 slices white bread	3 tbsp/45 mL extra-virgin olive oil
4 anchovies	1 tbsp/15 mL butter, for baking dish
4 cloves garlic	2 cups/500 mL milk
½ cup/125 mL pecorino toscano cheese	salt and pepper

Preheat oven to 375°F (190°C).

Bring a pot of salted water to a boil. Separate the cardoon stalks and rinse thoroughly under cold running water. Remove the tough, stringy outer ribs by peeling the cardoons as though they were potatoes. Cut the remaining stalks into 3-inch (7.5 cm) pieces and plunge into the boiling water. Once the water has returned to a boil, remove the cardoons. Drain and cool on paper towels.

Pulse the bread, anchovies, garlic, pecorino, parsley, and olive oil in a food processor until combined.

Place the cardoons in a buttered baking dish, lining them up tightly. Pour in the milk, season with salt and pepper, and bake for 20 minutes, or until the cardoons are soft.

Sprinkle the bread mixture on top and put the dish under the grill for 1–2 minutes, just until the topping is golden-crisp.

carote carmellate al limone
caramelized lemon carrots

Growing up in the country has its rewards. My home garden was always ready to give up seasonal delicacies, and carrots were one of them. I only had to scout the patch for the biggest fronds to pull up a tasty treat.

I recommend using small bunched carrots or a variety of heirloom carrots rather than large, thick carrots for this recipe. They can be cut or left whole, as I have done here.

Makes 4–6 servings

3 bunches carrots (approximately 20)	2 tbsp/30 mL lemon juice
1 tbsp/15 mL extra-virgin olive oil	1 cup/250 mL water
salt and pepper	1 tbsp/15 mL grated lemon zest
2 tbsp/30 mL honey	2 tbsp/30 mL Italian parsley

Wash and peel the carrots, leaving some of the green tops on.

Heat the olive oil in a sauté pan over medium heat. Add the carrots and season to taste with salt and pepper. Add the honey, lemon juice, and water; simmer until all the water has evaporated and the carrots are cooked. At this point the pan should be dry and the carrots will begin to caramelize. Let them brown, being careful not to let them burn. Add the lemon zest and parsley and toss to mix.

rapini con le acciughe
sautéed rapini with anchovies

"Eat it, it's good for you"—so my mother used to say when she served rapini (also known as rabe, rape, and canola). As with other bitter vegetables, I wasn't too crazy about rapini, but my tastes have since changed and now I love it. My clientele does too, and rapini will always be on the menu in one dish or another. The most popular is pasta with rapini and a generous grating of pecorino cheese.

I got the idea to add cream at a restaurant in Bari, where this is a traditional dish. The chef there told me that cream helps take away the rapini's bitterness by adding a mild sweetness.

Makes 4–6 servings

2 bunches rapini	1 red chilli pepper, chopped
4 tbsp/60 mL extra-virgin olive oil	salt and pepper
4 cloves garlic, crushed	½ cup/125 mL water
8 anchovy fillets, chopped	4 tbsp/60 mL heavy cream (optional)

Rinse the rapini under cold running water. Cut away the bottom 2 inches (5 cm) of the stems and discard. Chop the remaining rapini into 2-inch (5 cm) pieces.

Heat the olive oil in a skillet, add the garlic and sauté for 1 minute. Add the anchovies and chilli pepper, and cook until the anchovies have almost disintegrated. Add the rapini and season with a pinch of salt (just a pinch—the anchovies are already salty) and pepper. Pour in the water and cover with a tight-fitting lid. Cook the rapini for about 10 minutes, until soft, making sure it doesn't dry out too much.

If you wish, add the cream at the end of the cooking, once the other liquid has been absorbed or evaporated, and cook just long enough for the rapini to absorb the cream.

piselli al prosciutto e scalogno
fresh green peas with prosciutto and shallots

I remember as though it were yesterday being a young boy and having to eat green peas—the tough, discolored skin, a tasteless ingredient in a tough veal stew. I would pick each one out, hiding them in my pocket or throwing them around the room, angering my keepers. Of course, I am talking not about my parents but of summer camp. In retrospect, those were fun times—and I got over my hang-up about peas.

Makes 4–6 servings

5 slices prosciutto di Parma, about 4 oz/155 g in total	3 cups/750 mL fresh (or frozen) shelled green peas
1 tbsp/15 mL extra-virgin olive oil	½ cup/125 mL vegetable stock
2 tbsp/30 mL butter	salt and pepper
1 cup/250 mL finely sliced shallots	1 sprig mint, finely sliced

Chop the prosciutto into a fine julienne no longer than 1 inch (2.5 cm).

Heat the oil and butter in a sauté pan over medium heat. Add the prosciutto and sauté for 1–2 minutes. Stir in the shallots and cook for another minute. Add the peas and vegetable stock. Season to taste with salt and pepper, and cook until the peas are tender—about 5 minutes for fresh, 3 minutes for frozen. Stir in the mint and serve.

cavoletti alle pancetta e mandorle
brussels sprouts with pancetta and almonds

Many people avoid Brussels sprouts. Maybe the sulfurous odor turns them off, or maybe they have only ever eaten them overcooked, which gives the sprouts a bitter taste, or undercooked, and tasting too green. When cooked properly, Brussels sprouts are wonderful, and I love them. I think you will too, after you've tried this recipe.

Makes 4–6 servings

1 lb/500 g Brussels sprouts, halved	$\frac{1}{2}$ cup/125 mL chopped pancetta
1 tsp/5 mL vegetable oil	$\frac{1}{2}$ cup/125 mL skinless almonds
2 tbsp/30 mL butter	salt and pepper
2 cloves garlic, crushed	1 cup/250 mL water
2 shallots, finely minced	

Blanch the Brussels sprouts in a pot of boiling salted water for 2 minutes. Drain and cool on paper towels.

In the meantime, heat the oil and butter in a sauté pan over medium heat and sauté the garlic and shallots for 1 minute. Add the pancetta.

Crush the almonds slightly with a mallet to bring out the flavor and add them to the pan; sauté for about 1 minute. Add the Brussels sprouts, season to taste with salt and pepper, and pour in the water. Simmer until all the water has evaporated and the sprouts are cooked. Be careful not to overcook them or they will be mushy. ☕

fagiolini in salsa
green beans in savory vinaigrette

French beans are very thin green beans, often sold prepackaged. Although they cost a bit more than regular green beans, the taste is worth it. They are sometimes available in yellow (often known as wax beans), which also work well in this recipe.

This dish is best enjoyed at room temperature—perfect for summertime.

Makes 4–6 servings

1 lb/500 g French beans, or regular green beans if not available	2 tbsp/30 mL red wine vinegar
4 tbsp/60 mL extra-virgin olive oil	2 tbsp/30 mL tomato sauce
1 clove garlic, minced	salt and pepper
2 tbsp/30 mL minced shallots	2 tbsp/30 mL finely sliced basil

Boil the beans in salted water until they are done to your liking, and cool in ice water.

Heat 1 tbsp/15 mL olive oil in a skillet over medium heat. Add the garlic and shallots and cook until soft and translucent. Sprinkle the vinegar on top and cook until it evaporates. Immediately add the tomato sauce, season to taste with salt and pepper, and simmer for 1 minute. Stir in the basil and remove from heat. Set aside to cool.

Once the dressing has cooled, pour it over the beans, tossing to mix well. ☞

funghi al pomodoro
sautéed mushrooms with tomato sauce

One of the many good reasons to go for a walk in the woods is the pleasure of finding mushrooms. Of course, you or your companion must know which mushrooms to pick. Many times my father and I returned home from our walks with large amounts of mushrooms and big grins on our faces.

Makes 4–6 servings

1 cup/250 mL whole shiitake mushrooms

1 cup/250 mL oyster or king oyster mushrooms

1 cup/250 mL whole honey mushrooms

1 cup/250 mL whole chanterelle mushrooms

6 tbsp/90 mL extra-virgin olive oil

4 cloves garlic, crushed

4 shallots, thinly sliced

1 bay leaf

1 tsp/5 mL oregano

½ cup/125 mL chicken stock

½ cup/125 mL tomato puree

salt and pepper

Remove the stems from the shiitake mushrooms. Cut the oyster or king oyster mushrooms into strips and remove the hard parts of the stems. Separate the honey mushrooms. Clean the stems of the chanterelle mushrooms, rinse them with cold water, and dry thoroughly.

Heat the olive oil in a heavy-bottomed frying pan over high heat. Add the garlic, shallots, bay leaf, and oregano; sauté for 3–4 seconds. Before the vegetables become too golden, add the mushrooms and sauté for a few more seconds. Pour in the chicken stock and cook until the broth is absorbed or evaporates.

Add the tomato puree and season to taste with salt and pepper. Cook for 2 more minutes.

peperonata veneta
sautéed peppers

At the end of the summer, local markets are flooded with peppers (capsicums). These beautiful-tasting vegetables can be preserved easily by first roasting them and then either freezing or canning them. But before you do that, make yourself some peperonata—sautéed peppers. Use them as a hot garnish for roasted chicken or at room temperature as an antipasto or topping for bruschetta.

Makes 4–6 servings

3 red bell peppers (capsicums)	8 plum (Roma) tomatoes, peeled and seeded
2 yellow bell peppers (capsicums)	salt and pepper
1 green bell pepper (capsicum)	3 tbsp/45 mL red wine vinegar
2 medium onions	1 bunch basil, coarsely chopped
¼ cup/50 mL extra-virgin olive oil	1 bunch Italian parsley, coarsely chopped
4 cloves garlic, sliced	

Preheat the oven to 475°F (245°C). Roast the peppers (capsicums) under the grill, turning occasionally, until the skins are entirely blistered and blackened. Remove from the oven and place in a bowl. Cover the bowl with plastic wrap and set aside until cool. Once the bell peppers (capsicums) are cool, remove the skins and seeds, rinse gently, and cut the bell peppers (capsicums) into wedges. Set aside.

Remove the first layer from the onions and cut them into wedges (about 8 wedges per onion). Heat the olive oil in a medium saucepan. Sauté the onions and garlic lightly for 1–2 minutes. Add the bell peppers (capsicums) and tomatoes. Stir well and simmer, covered, for about 30 minutes, stirring occasionally to prevent sticking.

Season to taste with salt and pepper and add the vinegar. Cook for another 5 minutes, covered. Just before you turn off the heat under the pan, stir in the basil and parsley. 🍲

castagne e legumi arrosto
caramelized chestnuts and winter vegetables

I use fresh chestnuts as much as possible when they are available. In this recipe they are complemented by naturally sweet vegetables. This is definitely a winter vegetable dish, and the sweetness of the vegetables and the flavor combinations are sure to make it a favorite in your repertoire. I like to sprinkle good balsamic vinegar on top and sometimes add a chopped pear or apple to the mix. It is wonderful as an accompaniment to turkey, capon, lamb, or wild game.

Makes 4–6 servings

2 tbsp/30 mL butter

2 tbsp/30 mL extra-virgin olive oil

2 medium carrots, cut into small sticks

1 cup/250 mL cipolline (Italian pearl onions), peeled and blanched

4 cloves garlic, chopped

4 slices buttercup squash (pumpkin), peeled

1 fennel bulb, sliced into 4 pieces

2 cups/500 mL fresh chestnuts, peeled and blanched, or vacuum-packed chestnuts

salt and pepper

Heat the butter and olive oil in a heavy-bottomed pan over medium-low heat. Add the carrots and cipolline and sauté for 3–4 minutes. Add the garlic, squash (pumpkin), fennel, and chestnuts. Season to taste with salt and pepper and cook until tender, turning the vegetables over gently when one side has turned golden. Maintain the medium-low heat throughout the cooking process to allow the vegetables to caramelize without burning.

Note: If you prefer, bake the vegetables in a 375°F (190°C) oven for about 15–20 minutes, or until soft and golden.

gratin di verdure
vegetarian shepherd's pie

I created this dish for the hit TV series Restaurant Makeover, and I still get e-mails asking me for the recipe. It's a vegetarian reworking of the traditional shepherd's pie; if you omit the cheese, it will be sure to please any vegan guest at your dinner table.

Makes 8 servings

2 tbsp/30 mL extra-virgin olive oil

4 cloves garlic, crushed

1 cup/250 mL julienned onion

2 cups/500 mL white cabbage, shredded

½ cup/125 mL julienned carrots

1 cup/250 mL small cauliflower florets

1 cup/250 mL diced tomatoes

½ cup/125 mL canned chickpeas, drained

salt and pepper

1 tsp/5mL Cajun spice mix, or to taste

½ cup/125 mL green peas

½ cup/125 mL corn

2½ cups/625 mL mashed potato

1 cup/250 mL grated grana padano cheese

Preheat the oven to 375°F (190°C).

Heat the olive oil in a frying pan over high heat. Add the garlic, onion, cabbage, carrot, cauliflower, tomatoes, and chickpeas. Season to taste with salt, pepper, and Cajun spice. Cook for 2–3 minutes—you want to cook the vegetables quickly but not to overcook them. Place the vegetables in a casserole dish and spread them out evenly.

Combine the peas and corn and spread on top of the vegetables. Spread the mashed potato to cover the vegetables and top with the grana padano. Bake for 30 minutes or until the top is crisp.

dolci / sweets

dolci   sweets

frittelle di carnevale
carnival donuts

Who doesn't love carnival? From Venice to New Orleans to Rio de Janeiro, this festive season is celebrated with parties and good eats, donuts among them. Enjoy these fried treats on their own or filled with zabaglione (see page 188).

Makes 40 small donuts

½ cup/125 mL brandy	1½ cups/300 mL all-purpose (plain) flour, sifted
1 cup/250 mL raisins	
2 tbsp/30 mL sugar	4 large eggs
¼ tsp/2 mL salt	1 tsp/5 mL vanilla extract
¼ cup/50 mL butter	sunflower oil, for frying
1 cup/250 mL water	powdered sugar, for dusting

Pour the brandy over the raisins to moisten them. Set aside.

In a pot, combine the sugar, salt, butter, and water, and bring to a boil. Add the flour and beat with a wooden spoon. Turn the heat down to medium and cook until the dough forms a ball and comes away from the sides of the pot. Remove from the heat.

Add the vanilla extract and then the eggs, one by one, mixing well, until little bubbles form in the dough. Stir in the raisins. Scoop up the dough with a wet teaspoon to form small freeform donuts.

Pour sunflower oil into a deep, heavy-bottomed frying pan to about 1 inch (2.5 cm) deep and heat to 350°F (180°C). Put in as many donuts as will fit loosely, and fry until they are a deep golden color. Remove from the oil with a slotted spoon or skimmer and drain on paper towels. Continue deep-frying the donuts until all the dough is used up.

Once they are cool, dust the donuts with powdered sugar.

torta sabbiosa
lombardy sand cake

In my childhood home, weekends were awaited with anticipation. My mother spent all day Saturday preparing the pasta, meats, and desserts for Sunday lunch. This cake was always on the table, ready to be offered to visitors, and with luck we would have some left over for ourselves.

I like to serve this cake with fragole al balsamico and whipped cream on the side.

Makes 12 servings

1 cup/250 mL all-purpose (plain) flour	1 tbsp/15 mL good-quality vanilla extract
1 cup/250 mL potato starch	grated zest of 1 lemon
1 tsp/5 mL baking soda	grated zest of 1 orange
¼ tsp/1 mL baking powder	2 tbsp/30 mL orange liqueur
1½ cups/375 mL butter, at room temperature	4 eggs, separated
	1 whole egg
2½ cups/550 mL sugar	powdered sugar, for dusting

Preheat the oven to 350°F (180°C).

In a medium bowl, sift together the flour, potato starch, baking soda, and baking powder.

Whip the butter with the sugar and vanilla extract to a creamy consistency. Stir in the lemon and orange zest and the liqueur. Add the egg yolks and whole egg, one by one, mixing well. Gradually add the flour mixture, mixing well to incorporate.

Whip the egg whites until soft peaks form. Gently fold into the batter, working with a spatula from the bottom of the bowl to the top, until well incorporated.

Butter and flour a 10- or 12-inch (25 or 30 cm) springform pan. Pour in the cake batter and level with a spatula or the back of a spoon. Bake for about 1 hour, or until a toothpick inserted in the center comes out clean. Do not open the oven door for the first 40 minutes of baking.

Remove the cake from the oven and allow to cool completely before turning out of the pan. Dust the cake with powdered sugar before serving.

coppa al caffè
coffee parfait

Trattoria dall'Amelia had one dessert that was always on my danger list: coffee parfait. I often saw Chef check the numbers after I had been in the walk-in fridge.

This parfait is a quick dessert to prepare for a large group of people. Long, slender glasses are ideal serving dishes, as they show off the attractive layers of the parfait. If you don't have stemware, get creative— use glass bowls or ice cream coupes, or whatever you have on hand.

Makes 4 servings

5 egg yolks	2 tsp/10 mL instant coffee powder
¼ cup/75 mL sugar	1 cup/250 mL chocolate sauce
4 tbsp/60 mL coffee liqueur	dark chocolate, for garnish
1 lb/500 g good-quality mascarpone cheese	

Place a medium bowl in a large, shallow pan of hot water. Put the egg yolks in the bowl and whip in the sugar and coffee liqueur until the mixture is pale and very thick. When lifted out with the beater, the batter should fall back onto the surface in a ribbon and sit for a few seconds before sinking back in. This process will cook the egg yolks. Set aside to cool.

Add the mascarpone and coffee powder to the eggs. Using an electric beater, whip until stiff peaks form. Be careful not to over-whip the cheese, or it will separate.

Pour a layer of chocolate sauce into a serving glass, add a scoop of the cheese mixture, another layer of chocolate, and another scoop of cheese. Continue layering until the glass is full; there should be at least five layers. Fill all the serving glasses this way and refrigerate for at least 1 hour.

Top with shavings of dark chocolate.

pere al balsamico con caprino al miele

balsamic roasted pears with whipped goat cheese

A common sight in Cremona's fruit markets is baked fruit and vegetables—from pears to apples to beetroots—making it easy for home cooks to prepare all sorts of dishes. For me, nothing finishes a great meal better than roasted fruit.

Makes 4 servings

2 tbsp/30 mL unsalted butter	4 oz/115 g creamy goat cheese, at room temperature
4 firm, ripe Bosc pears, halved lengthwise and cored	5 tbsp/75 mL wildflower honey
3 tbsp/45 mL balsamic vinegar	¼ tsp/2 mL freshly cracked black pepper

Preheat the oven to 450°F (230°C).

Melt the butter in an 8-inch (20 cm) glass baking dish on the middle rack of the oven, for about 3 minutes.

Arrange the pears, cut side down, in the butter, and roast until tender, about 20 minutes. Pour the vinegar over the pears and roast for 5 more minutes. Transfer the pears to serving plates, cut side up.

In a metal bowl, whip the goat cheese and 1 tbsp/15 mL honey with an electric mixer or beater until fluffy. Using a warm spoon, place a dollop of cheese in the center of each pear half. Drizzle the baking juices over the pears.

Top the pears and cheese with the remaining 4 tbsp/60 mL honey and freshly cracked black pepper.☕

torta di mele di maddalena
maddalena's apple cake

My sister-in-law, an excellent cook, often bakes a cake "just in case we have visitors"—a good plan, except that the cake is gobbled up before she has a chance to serve it to any guests. My kids and my wife love this moist cake, and this is my take on it. The apricot jelly glaze will give the cake a nice shine.

Makes 12 servings

2 lb/1 kg green or sour baking apples (approximately 6 apples)

juice of 2 lemons

1½ cups/425 mL all-purpose (plain) flour

2 tsp/10 mL baking powder (or packaged Italian yeast if available)

pinch of salt

½ cup/150 mL butter, at room temperature

½ cup/175 mL sugar

1 tbsp/15 mL vanilla extract

1 tbsp/15 mL grated lemon zest

3 eggs

2 tbsp/30 mL milk, plus more as needed

2 tbsp/30 mL melted butter

3 tbsp/45 mL apricot jelly

2 tbsp/30 mL water

powdered sugar, for garnish

Preheat the oven to 350°F (180°C).

Peel, core, and quarter the apples. Cut each quarter in half so that each apple yields eight wedges. Sprinkle with the lemon juice to prevent discoloring, and set aside.

In a medium bowl, sift the flour, baking powder, and salt.

In a metal bowl, cream the butter with the sugar, vanilla extract, and lemon zest, using an electric mixer. Add the eggs one at a time, whipping until the batter is light and fluffy. Turn the mixer to slow and add about half of the flour mixture and 1 tbsp/15 mL milk. Mix well, then add the rest of the flour mixture. If the batter is too thick, add more milk—it should be fluffy, not runny.

Pour the batter into a greased 10- or 12-inch (25 or 30 cm) springform cake pan and level with a spatula or the back of a spoon. Arrange the apple wedges on top in a pattern, leaving about $\frac{1}{4}$ inch (1 cm) around the sides to allow for the batter to expand. Brush the apples with the melted butter. Bake for 45–50 minutes, or until a toothpick inserted in the center comes out clean. Remove the cake from the oven and let cool for 10–15 minutes before turning out onto a cake rack to cool completely.

In a saucepan over medium-low heat, dissolve the apricot jelly in the water. Brush over the top of the cooled cake. Finish the cake by dusting powdered sugar around the edges.

biscuit del dondeo
chestnut and chocolate semifreddo

Dondeo is a famous pastry shop in Cremona. It opened in 1926, and my grandfather used to sell milk, eggs, and fruit to it. Among its many high-quality pastries and famous cappuccino, its chestnut and chocolate semifreddo stands out; it has been part of our family celebrations for as long as I can remember. This is my version.

Makes 12 servings

5 eggs, separated

1 cup/250 mL sugar

1½ cups/375 mL whipping cream

½ cup/175 mL marrons glacé (candied chestnuts), chopped

½ cup/125 mL good-quality chocolate shavings

1 lb/500 g store-bought meringue

2 tbsp/30 mL powdered sugar

Place a medium bowl in a large, shallow pan of hot water, and whisk together the egg yolks and ¼ cup/50 mL sugar in the bowl until thick and fluffy. Lay plastic wrap directly on top of the mixture and refrigerate until cold.

Whip the cream and gently fold it into the egg mixture. Beat the egg whites until soft peaks form. Gradually beat in the remaining ½ cup/175 mL sugar until stiff, glossy peaks form. Gently fold into the egg yolk mixture. Fold in the chestnuts and chocolate shavings.

Crumble half of the meringue into the bottom of a 10-inch (25 cm) cake mold, pour in the batter, and crumble the remaining meringue on top, pressing down gently to even out the filling. Wrap with plastic wrap and place in the freezer for at least 6 hours.

Remove from the cake mold and sprinkle with powdered sugar to finish.

risotto al cioccolato
chocolate risotto

This may seem strange at first, but—trust me!—everyone loves it.
Chocolate risotto is a luscious version of chocolate rice pudding.
It's the perfect end to a meal that doesn't contain too much starch.

Makes 4 servings

2 tbsp/30 mL unsalted butter	1 cup/250 mL milk
1 cup/250 mL vialone nano or other risotto rice, unwashed	½ cup/125 mL heavy cream
1 vanilla bean, split	½ cup/75 mL white sugar
2 tbsp/30 mL rum	1 tsp/5 mL grated orange zest
2 cups/500 mL water	1 tsp/5 mL grated lemon zest
	½ lb/125 g dark chocolate, chopped

Melt the butter in a saucepan over very high heat. Add the rice and stir
continuously until the rice is very hot but not browned. Add the vanilla
bean, rum, and water; cook until almost all the liquid has evaporated.

Add a small amount of the milk and stir until it has been absorbed by
the rice. Continue to add the milk in small amounts until it has all been
absorbed and the rice is cooked. This process will take 15–18 minutes
in total.

Remove the pan from the heat and add the cream, sugar, orange and
lemon zest, and chocolate. Stir well to incorporate all the ingredients.
Serve at once.

tortino di frutta di bosco
mixed berry pudding

This is one recipe that really kicks. I originally wanted a cake that had apple chunks in it and was very moist, almost wet. I fiddled around and eventually came up with this—out with the apple and in with the berries!

This pudding bakes best in individual molds, so a large muffin pan is ideal to use. If you don't have one, use a ring mold or Bundt pan.

Makes 6–8 servings

butter, for greasing the mold	¼ tsp/2 mL baking soda
flour, for dusting the mold	¼ tsp/1 mL salt
½ cup/125 mL vegetable oil	½ cup/125 mL diced strawberries
1 cup/250 mL sugar	½ cup/125 mL blueberries
¼ tsp/2 mL vanilla extract	½ cup/125 mL raspberries
1 egg	
1 cup/250 mL all-purpose (plain) flour	

Preheat the oven to 350°F (180°C).

Generously butter and flour the cups of a large muffin tin (or use paper liners) or a 10-inch (25 cm) ring mold or Bundt pan. This is an important step, as the batter is very sticky.

Combine the oil and sugar, stirring until they have a creamy consistency. Add the vanilla extract and egg, and mix well.

In a medium bowl, combine the flour, baking soda, and salt. Fold in the creamed sugar mixture. Add the strawberries and then the blueberries. Stir in the raspberries very gently. Pour the batter into the baking dish and bake for 50 minutes, if using a cake pan, or 10–15 minutes, if using a muffin tin. A toothpick inserted in the center of the cake should come out dry.

latte fritto al limoncello
fried milk bites with limoncello

Fried milk is perhaps more Spanish than Italian, but it is becoming increasingly popular on the dessert menus of Italian restaurants. This version is made with Limoncello, a lemon liqueur made in the south of Italy. When I started making this dessert at Mistura, I had no idea how it would be received, but so many of my customers like it, it's been on the menu for years.

Makes 8 servings

For lemon cream:	For frying:
2 cups/500 mL milk	sunflower oil, for frying
6 tbsp/90 mL sugar	2 tbsp/30 mL granulated sugar, or as needed
grated zest of 2 lemons	
1 tsp/5 mL vanilla extract	2 eggs
6 tbsp/90 mL all-purpose (plain) flour	flour, for dredging
3 tbsp/45 mL cornstarch (cornflour)	
6 tbsp/90 mL Limoncello liqueur	
juice of 1 lemon	
4 egg yolks	

To prepare the lemon cream, boil 1 $\frac{1}{2}$ cups/375 mL milk in a saucepan with the sugar, half of the lemon zest, and the vanilla extract.

In a bowl, combine the flour with the cornstarch (cornflour). Add the remaining $\frac{1}{2}$ cup/125 mL milk, Limoncello, lemon juice, and egg yolks. Pour in the scalded milk, mixing well and quickly so that no lumps form and the consistency is creamy.

Pour the mixture back into the pan and boil until it becomes solid, just a few minutes. Immediately spread the mixture to about $\frac{1}{2}$ inch (2 cm) thick on a tray lined with waxed paper. Cool completely, for as long as 8–12 hours if possible. When it is ready, cut the cooled cream into diamond shapes.

Pour sunflower oil into a deep, heavy-bottomed frying pan to about 1 inch (2.5 cm) deep and heat to 350°F (180°C).

In the meantime, mix the sugar with the remaining lemon zest. Beat the eggs in a bowl. Dredge the lemon cream diamonds with flour on a plate, shake off any excess, and dip them in the beaten eggs, coating well. Again dredge the diamonds with the flour, shake well to remove any excess, and fry in the oil until crisp and golden.

Drain the fried cream on paper towels for a few seconds, then roll in the lemon sugar and transfer to a plate. Serve the diamonds warm on their own or with fruit compote.

zabaglione classico
classic zabaglione

This is by far the simplest dessert to prepare, and so versatile. Serve as a side dish with panettone, stollen, or kugelhopf. Add some berries if you wish to lighten the flavor. Or let the zabaglione cool, fold in meringue and whipped cream, and freeze to make a semifreddo. Many more recipes come to mind, but really the easiest way to enjoy it is just as it is. Add a couple of cookies on the side and you're done.

Makes 4 servings

4 egg yolks

4 tbsp/60 mL sugar

½ cup/125 mL Marsala

1 tbsp/15 mL cocoa powder

In a metal bowl, beat the egg yolks with the sugar until the yolks are pale. Add the Marsala and mix well.

In the bottom of a double boiler, bring water to just below the boiling point (boiling water will make the eggs taste burned). Add the egg mixture to the top and whip for 2–3 minutes, until stiff peaks form.

Serve dusted with cocoa powder.

In a metal bowl, beat the egg yolks with the sugar until the yolks are pale. Add the Marsala and mix well.

In the bottom of a double boiler, bring water to just below the boiling point (boiling water will make the eggs taste burned). Add the egg mixture to the top and whip for 2–3 minutes, until stiff peaks form.

Serve dusted with cocoa powder.

index